AI Pluralism

P. Anand Rao
Editor

AI Pluralism

Fostering Diversity and Dialogue in Artificial Intelligence

palgrave
macmillan

Editor
P. Anand Rao
Communication and Digital Studies
University of Mary Washington
Fredericksburg, VA, USA

ISBN 978-3-032-06557-5 ISBN 978-3-032-06558-2 (eBook)
https://doi.org/10.1007/978-3-032-06558-2

This Palgrave Macmillan imprint is published by the registered company Springer Nature Switzerland AG.
The registered company address is: Gewerbestrasse 11, 6330 Cham, Switzerland

Contents

PART I

Theoretical Foundations

CHAPTER 1

Introduction

Stefan Bauschard and G. Thomas Goodnight

Abstract From Hiroshima's mushroom cloud to today's cloud-based algorithms, this chapter frames artificial intelligence as the next decisive rupture in human history. It recounts how the 1945 atomic blast exposed science's capacity to annihilate, turning physicists into prophets and politics into existential calculus, and argues that AI detonates similar forces in code: concentrating power, redefining security, and challenging democratic agency. The "AI race" is mapped across corporations and nations that seek technological, economic, and military dominance through frontier models, multimodal agents, and humanoid robots, while export controls and military–tech fusion harden geopolitical stakes. Yet the authors reject a monolithic path toward artificial superintelligence. Instead, they propose "AI pluralism," a design philosophy that fosters diverse, interacting intelligences whose dialectical exchange reduces risk, corrects error, and preserves human autonomy. Drawing on pragmatism, rhetorical theory, and empirical safety research, they outline protocols—diversity, egalitarianism, and synergy—that can embed debate, transparency, and distributed oversight into both virtual and physical AI systems. The

S. Bauschard (✉) • G. T. Goodnight
21st Century Forensics, University of Southern California,
Los Angeles, CA, USA
e-mail: stefanbauschard@globalacademic.org; gtg@usc.edu

P. A. Rao (ed.), *AI Pluralism*,
https://doi.org/10.1007/978-3-032-06558-2_1

chapter previews contributions from philosophy, computer science, education, rhetoric, and policy that together build a roadmap for pluralistic governance, urging an ecological rather than imperial vision of intelligence for an age of ambient machine minds. It closes by inviting readers into this vital dialogue.

Keywords Artificial Intelligence (AI) • AI Pluralism • Artificial General Intelligence (AGI) • Artificial Narrow Intelligence (ANI) • Artificial Superintelligence (ASI) • Autonomous Agents • Humanoid Robotics • Safety Governance • Dialectical Debate • Democratic Oversight • Pragmatism • Diversity in Intelligence • Synergy Protocols • Fourth Industrial Revolution • Fifth Industrial Revolution

1.1 The Quest for Dominance

On the morning of 6 August 1945, a single flash above Hiroshima shattered the boundary between laboratory and battlefield. In less than a second, a city of 350,000 people was reduced to ash and silence; more than 80,000 lives were extinguished instantly, and tens of thousands more would succumb to radiation in the months that followed. For the first time, a purely human invention threatened the species that invented it. The mushroom cloud was not merely a military milestone but a philosophical rupture—proof that scientific progress could just as readily annihilate as enlighten. Overnight, physicists became prophets, politicians confronted existential calculus, and ordinary citizens discovered that the fate of millions could hinge on decisions made in secret rooms.

Eighty years later, artificial intelligence (AI) is staging a quieter but no less consequential detonation—this time in code rather than uranium. Like physics and the atom, AI started with a small number of elite researchers thinking in new ways. John McCarthy is said to have originated the term in 1956 in a paper at a Dartmouth meeting (McCorduck, 2004). Just as physicists, beginning with Einstein's 1905 papers, eventually harnessed atomic energy—with all its constructive and destructive potential—AI researchers have methodically assembled knowledge across decades to create systems that now reshape entire industries and even humanity itself.

AI has been heralded by Google's Sundar Pichai (in Fridman, 2025) as "more profound than fire or electricity," a technology that will be able to develop itself and whose ripple effects will penetrate every layer of society, from gene editing and climate modeling to battlefield autonomy and democratic protocols. And just as the atom bomb reaped destruction as a result of its exponential cataclysm caused by atoms crashing into each other, so too might AI wreak havoc as it rapidly intertwines itself in every fragment of our existence through distributed "detonations" of code running in real-time across the planet.

The existential calculations that scientists of the nuclear Manhattan Project (1942–1947) wrestled with—*who controls the knowledge, how it might be weaponized, who uses it to obtain dominance, and whether safeguards can keep pace—preoccupied* generations. The nuclear arms race was ultimately a race to dominate geopolitics through sheer destructive capacity, locking in hierarchies defined by who held the most powerful weapons, as seen when the US and Soviet Union maintained tens of thousands of warheads and conducted provocative exercises like Able Archer–83 that nearly triggered nuclear war through mistaken signals.

As with nuclear power, scientists and governments knew what was coming with AI. Investment firms readied capital shifts. The elites assembled networks of factories and corporations to turn AI from an announcement to a participatory narrative for public acceptance. Henry Kissinger put the story out for everyone in the autumn of 2022: "Created by humans, AI should be overseen by humans. But in our time, one of AI's challenges is that the skills and resources required to create it are not inevitably paired with the philosophical perspective to understand its broader implications" (Kissinger et al., 2021). Thoughtful pairing, opportunism, or obsolescence were the choices in play. The opportunity was nothing less than the chance to develop "Machines with Loving Grace" (Amodei, 2024).

1.2 The AI Race for Control

While AI had been under development for decades, the launch of a working generative model, ChatGPT3.5, that was accessible to anyone, stunned the world and accelerated investment. In late 2022, ChatGPT broke records as the AI platform reached 1 million users in less than two weeks. It now has close to 1 billion weekly users (Statista Research Department, 2025).

Despite distinct strategies, leading AI companies align on core milestones: fluid multimodal interfaces, autonomous agent architectures with reasoning and planning capabilities, and artificial general intelligence featuring common sense, adaptability, and self-awareness. Yet AI concepts remain fluid and speculative—AI, Artificial General Intelligence (AGI), and Artificial Superior Intelligence (ASI) are aspirational terms open to interpretation rather than clear boundaries. These capabilities supposedly progress from Artificial Narrow Intelligence (exceeding human abilities in specific domains, already achieved) through AGI (human equivalence) to ASI (beyond human capacities). Rather than defining limits, these terms describe varied computer-generated, automated digital networks.

These AI technologies can augment human capabilities—sometimes enhancing our sensory perception, other times creating autonomous or semi-autonomous agents that operate in both digital and physical environments. They are also entities we will interact with. The engineer- promoter Klaus Schmidt (2025) writes, "The possibilities of billions of people connected by mobile devices, with unprecedented processing power, storage capacity, and access to knowledge, are unlimited."

Although AI has shot to the forefront, these speculative visions gained institutional momentum when Klaus Schwab announced the "Fourth Industrial Revolution"at the 2016 World Economic Forum (WEF). He declared that AI "is evolving at an exponential rather than a linear pace.

Moreover, it is disrupting almost every industry in every country" (Schwab, 2016), describing an unprecedented convergence of AI with robotics, biotechnology, quantum computing, and other emerging technologies. The WEF has since become a key venue where business and political leaders translate these technological narratives into governance frameworks, industry partnerships, and investment priorities that shape global AI development.

AI has emerged from the convergence of communications, computer science, engineering, social sciences, neuroscience, and quantum machine learning—a synthesis that now accelerates discovery across all these fields. By enabling faster analysis, more efficient processing, and the handling of vast datasets, both natural and synthetic, AI promises to transform entire systems of production, management, and governance. As humans begin to merge with AI—through brain- computer interfaces, AI-augmented cognition, and ambient intelligence—we may already be entering a Fifth Industrial Revolution, or even a Sixth, where the boundaries between human and machine become entirely blurred. Just as the rise of the

Industrial Revolution would impact us in a variety of constructive and destructive ways, so too would AI system changes impact all of humanity. This convergence reflects a shared vision of scaling superintelligent capabilities across billions of users, serving markets from consumer applications to defense contracting. The prospect of 30 billion superintelligent agents operating globally illustrates the magnitude of this transformation.

While some predict digital superintelligence as soon as 2026 (Amodei; Musk), advances are not limited to replicating human brainpower. Physical AI—the melding of AI with robotics—is a pivotal frontier. Companies and governments are racing to build humanoid and domain-specific robots that can perceive, move, manipulate, and collaborate. Notable examples include Tesla's Optimus, Figure AI's Fig. 02, and Agility Robotics' Digit (Kall, 2025). These robots, trained with large vision-language models and simulations, adapt to real-world environments with minimal manual coding.

These singular, co-opting narratives of the human knowledge processes should be addressed with caution, however. The stories do have examples of wonders, such as defeating a chess champion, the discovery of gene folds, or winning a public debate. These examples, however, are accompanied by definitions that generalize to an elite realm without access to most users and, like Oppenheimer's broken mirror, reflect disagreement on some basic ideas. These few examples a fortiori present themselves as harbingers of even greater marvels to come. Promotions take on the tone of a magic show. However, thousands of YouTube discussions get into comparing development and particular system attributes. The AI company and its processes and products are said to be growing, improving, and tending to general human intelligence soon. Further, the floating signifiers that rename AI projects as a future of riches do have a catch; the public must endure the instabilities, limits, and lack of account in the present (Amodei, 2024; Diamandis, 2025). Mistakes will be corrected. Why? By whom? How?

The AI race represents a fundamental struggle for dominance across technological, economic, and geopolitical dimensions. Companies compete to define humanity's interface with intelligence itself, while nations pursue AI leadership for economic supremacy, military advantage, and global influence through massive investments and protective regulations. Beyond commercial interests, controlling advanced AI systems grants unprecedented power over information flow, decision-making, and social organization. The stakes are existential: achieving breakthrough capabilities first could establish irreversible advantages in shaping civilization's trajectory, making this less about innovation and more about securing permanent control over humanity's future power structures.

The US is reinforcing its AI lead over China through regulatory and strategic measures. In June 2025, senior executives from Palantir, Meta, OpenAI, and Thinking Machine Labs were commissioned as reservist lieutenant colonels in the Army Reserve's Detachment 201, also known as the Executive Innovation Corps, bringing tech expertise directly into military planning (The Week, 2025). Policymakers are even considering a "Manhattan Project–style" initiative to achieve supremacy in artificial general intelligence (AGI), although export controls on semiconductors may be accelerating China's AI progress—January 2025's DeepSeek R1 model reportedly performs only months behind US counterparts (CNN, 2025).

But beneath the geopolitical maneuvering and corporate competition lies a more fundamental question about human experience itself. Living among such ambient, ever-present intelligences raises qualitatively new civic challenges: how do human communities share space, authority, and even consciousness with entities that are neither mere tools nor fully autonomous peers, and how can we avoid conflict driven by attempts to dominate? Unlike earlier machines, large-scale AI systems do not occupy discrete factories or devices; they operate as diffuse layers of cognition, recommending news, policing content, orchestrating logistics, tutoring children, negotiating stock trades, and, increasingly, controlling physical robots in homes and streets. Their decisions are continuous, probabilistic, and often inscrutable, shaping outcomes long before humans notice a pattern or can exercise oversight. To coexist sustainably, societies will need mechanisms that make these invisible actors legible and contestable: *pluralistic agent ensembles* that critique one another in real-time, and public institutions capable of mediating disputes between humans and machines.

Rinse and repeat. Overnight, physicists became prophets, politicians confronted existential calculus, and ordinary citizens discovered that the fate of millions could hinge on decisions made in secret rooms. *Who controls the knowledge, how it might be weaponized, who uses it to obtain dominance, and how can we keep it safe?*

Rising to the stakes of this magnitude demands an intellectual upgrade: we need theories that treat intelligence as ecology rather than artifact, emphasizing diversity, contestation, and negotiated coexistence. Instead of assuming a single, ever-larger, dominating model can safely mediate all human affairs. Just as liberal democracies disperse power to protect freedom, pluralistic AI architectures disperse cognition to preserve truth and human agency, offering a roadmap for living among ubiquitous, rapidly evolving machine minds. AI has a trust problem (Chakravorty, 2024). Oddly, these are all qualities that humans develop through experience into common sense. Protreptic generalized affiliations (e.g., norms, values, ideals) with common-sense judgments constitute ways of knowing. Practical knowledge, though local, is representative in a variety of protocols in diverse cultures across time and geographies. The practical thinking characteristic of our species is, by virtue of its evolving nature, pluralistic.

1.3 AI Pluralism

1.3.1 Why AI Pluralism?

Just as the atomic bomb was not merely a weapon but a symbol of political will fused with scientific might, AI represents more than just a technological breakthrough—it is a new lever of geopolitical and epistemic power. In the aftermath of Hiroshima, the world was forced to reckon with the reality that scientific innovation could instantly rewrite the rules of global order. Today, AI has begun to carry a similar weight. Its capacity to centralize authority—over economies, militaries, narratives, and minds—echoes the Cold War's logic of mutually assured dominance, only faster, quieter, and more deeply woven into the infrastructure of daily life. The pursuit of AI dominance, especially at the frontier-model level, becomes not just a competition of systems but of values: whose intelligence gets to define what is rational, what is ethical, and what is true.

This book introduces and develops a different approach: AI pluralism. Rather than pursuing a monolithic vision of artificial intelligence, AI pluralism embraces differentiation of AI agents in terms of their perspectives, capabilities, and even their architectural foundations. It envisions a landscape where multiple AI systems, each with different capabilities and viewpoints, can engage in genuine dialectical exchange, producing more robust, transparent, and safe outcomes than any single system could achieve alone.

Pluralism answers: *How should we design systems governing our digital and physical realities?* AI pluralism advocates cultivating diverse intelligences—each trained differently, operating from distinct assumptions, and held accountable through structured dialogue—rather than building a single dominant intelligence.

This approach employs common-sense protocols manifesting across personal, professional, and public expression, addressing micro to macro scales. Common-sense norms and values aren't finite; humans adaptively integrate cognition, affective affiliation, and intersubjective coordination across varied subjectivities. Human cultures remain pluralistic as languages evolve through generational experimentation. AI serves as an affordance for individuals navigating occasions—historical moments where control systems meet rising communication needs among minds working together and in tension. These protocols work with energies to achieve integration and dispersal of cognition, authoritative gesture, disguise, and display across different subjectivities. Diverse intelligences are inherited from different cultures and remake themselves through each individual, group, and generation's achievements and limitations.

This work begins a counter-story to the AI narrative of singularity. We select three common- sense protocols to begin building practical alternatives to the explosive narrative of a promised AI future.

- **Diversity** ensures that AI agents are not carbon copies of one another. They should be shaped by varied training data, distinct model architectures, or even divergent embodied experiences, allowing them to represent a true spectrum of perspectives.
- **Egalitarianism** rejects the notion that sheer computational power or corporate resources should determine whose AI has authority. Instead, pluralism seeks ways of interacting that prevent any one system from monopolizing influence or silencing alternatives.
- **Synergy** is the engine of the pluralist model. Rather than issuing unchallenged outputs, AI systems must engage in real dialectical exchange—questioning, testing, and debating each other's claims before those claims are allowed to shape human lives.

The design principles call for protocols that become tested, evaluated, borrowed, adapted, and followed to ripeness. The industry posts and follows benchmarks to yield information on industry-selected criteria for success. Civil society requires protocols for democratic assessment where time, resources, and needs are accorded in ways that sustain legitimacy, repair from catastrophe, and allocate advantage and risk in ways that are fair and just.

Philosophies constitute cultural resources to draw from in creating alternative AI narratives. Pluralism has deep philosophical roots, particularly in American pragmatism and the work of Alfred North Whitehead (1929). This tradition emphasizes "becoming" and "concrescence"—the coming together of elements in different ways—ideas that resonate strongly with the challenges we face in AI development today. Pluralism in this sense is not merely theoretical but inherently practical, focused on how differences productively interact within systems to generate new possibilities.

1.4 The Technological Edge of Pluralism

Pluralism is not mere ethics-washing; it is a performance strategy. Empirical work shows that models trained to debate one another expose reasoning errors, reduce hallucinations, and generate more reliable answers. Architectural diversity—LLMs, state-space models, vision- language transformers—mirrors biological ecosystems where specialization breeds resilience. Adversarial red-teaming and multiple agent "personas" uncover security exploits that a monolithic tester misses. Pluralism thus advances safety and capability in tandem (Asad et al., 2025).

1.4.1 From Virtual Minds to Physical Bodies

The pluralistic frontier now extends into "physical AI": robots that sense, move, and act alongside us. When these embodied agents negotiate warehouse lanes, elder-care routines, or disaster zones, pluralistic coordination matters even more—mechanical failures carry physical risk. Embedding debate, diversity, and distributed oversight inside fleets of autonomous machines is therefore an urgent safety requirement, not an academic luxury (Rahwan et al., 2019).

1.4.2 Bridging Humanities and Sciences

By speaking to this diverse audience, we hope to facilitate the cross-disciplinary conversation necessary for AI pluralism to flourish. Too often, technical discussions of AI proceed in isolation from humanistic concerns, while humanistic critiques lack engagement with technical realities.

This book attempts to bridge that gap, creating space for genuine dialogue across disciplinary boundaries.

1.5 The Structure of This Book

This volume brings together perspectives from computer science, education, communication, and philosophy to provide a comprehensive examination of AI pluralism. It moves from theoretical foundations to practical applications, offering insights for researchers, developers, educators, and policymakers.

Human civilization has always evolved through *intersubjectivity*—through minds encountering other minds, cultures testing the limits of their assumptions, and knowledge advancing through contest and dialogue. Pluralism, whether in politics, art, or science, depends on ***bounded multiplicity***: perspectives that are partial but in conversation. Yet, as humans and machines become increasingly hybrid—entangled in shared cognition and co-evolving feedback loops—the danger of homogenization deepens. If both human and synthetic minds are trained within the same cognitive architectures, we lose not only competition but the dialectic of difference that sustains understanding itself.

AI pluralism insists that intelligence, like democracy, requires a chorus rather than a soloist. Multiple AIs—divergent in architecture, value alignment, and interpretive style—should not merely coexist but **argue with one another**, just as hybrid human-machine intelligences must remain distinct enough to challenge one another's reasoning. The goal is not only to keep power distributed but to preserve a field of *productive friction* in which each intelligence—organic, synthetic, or composite—sees what others miss. Protocols emanate from dialectics of sameness and difference—meaning that safety, creativity, and ethics emerge only when systems must negotiate across boundaries. Monolithic AI reduces uncertainty; pluralistic and hybrid AI learn to live with it. In that tension—between collaboration and contestation—lies resilience. Truth, in this new landscape, will not be a static database but the *ongoing negotiation among diverse and entangled intelligences.*

To build such a world is not to control intelligence but to **design for coexistence**—among humans, machines, and the hybrids now forming between them. A pluralistic AI ecology mirrors the pluralistic foundations of human life: distributed, self-correcting, never finished. It demands fostering many epistemologies—symbolic, neural, embodied, moral—each evolving in dialogue, each a check against the hubris of certainty. Just as democracy depends on dissent to stay alive, AI must depend on plurality and hybridity to stay human. In the end, AI pluralism is not simply a technical safeguard; it is a civilizational choice—to let *difference and hybridity* endure as the conditions of both freedom and wisdom.

The book begins with this introduction, establishing the fundamental concepts and necessity of AI pluralism. Chapter 2, authored by John Hines, delves into the philosophical foundations of AI pluralism, examining its roots in American pragmatism and providing the conceptual framework that guides our approach. Chapter 3, authored by P. Anand Rao, examines how rhetorical argumentation can enhance the explainability and contestability of AI systems—key requirements for meaningful pluralism.

Chapter 4, written by Devin Gonier, bridges theory and practice by exploring technical frameworks for implementing AI pluralism, including innovative training methodologies and architectural approaches.

Chapter 5, by Stefan Bauschard, explores debate and dialectical reasoning as safety mechanisms in pluralistic AI systems.

Chapter 6, authored by Alan Coverstone, examines how AI pluralism can revolutionize educational practices by embracing Howard Gardner's theory of. multiple intelligences.

Chapter 7, by G. Thomas Goodnight, examines the manifestation of AI pluralism in the takeoff of AI throughout epistemic communities. These groups grow locally, nationally, and internationally to address the ever-growing civic demands of AI and urban life.

Throughout these chapters, you'll find a consistent thread: the recognition that artificial intelligence need not—and indeed should not—develop along a single, monolithic path. Instead, we can cultivate a rich ecosystem of AI systems that, through their diversity and interaction, enhance human capability and agency rather than diminishing it.

As we stand at this crucial moment in AI development, we invite you to consider the possibilities offered by AI pluralism—a path that embraces the full complexity of intelligence and creates space for genuine dialogue between human and artificial minds. This book represents not an end point but a beginning—the opening of a conversation we hope will continue to evolve and expand as AI development progresses.

References

Amodei, D. (2024, October 12). *Machines of loving grace: How AI could transform the world for the better* [Essay]. *Anthropic.* Retrieved from https://www.anthropic.com/essay

Asad, A., Obadinma, S., Shayanfar, R., & Zhu, X. (2025, June 4). *RedDebate: Safer responses through multi-agent red-teaming debates* [Preprint]. arXiv. https://doi.org/10.48550/arXiv.2506.11083 kodemsecurity.com+10

Chakravorty, B. (2024). AI's trust problem. *Harvard Business Review*. https://hbr.org/2024/05/ais-trust-problem

CNN. (2025, May 29). *China's DeepSeek releases update to AI model that sent US shares tumbling*.https://www.cnn.com/2025/05/29/tech/china-deepseek-releases-update-intl-hnk

Diamandis, P. H. (2025, April 15). *Metatrends shaping the next decade. Diamandis.com.* Retrieved from https://www.diamandis.com/blog/metatrends-shaping-decade

Kissinger, H. A., Schmidt, E., & Huttenlocher, D. (2021). *The Age of AI: And our human future*. Little.

Rahwan, I., Cebrian, M., Obradovich, N., Bongard, J., Bonnefon, J. F., Breazeal, C., et al. (2019). Machine behaviour. *Nature, 568*(7753), 477–486. https://doi.org/10.1038/s41586-019-1138-y

Fridman, L. (Host). (2025, June 5). *#471—Sundar Pichai: CEO of Google and Alphabet* [Audio podcast episode]. In the *Lex Fridman Podcast*. https://www.youtube.com/watch?v=9V6tWC4CdFQ

McCorduck, P. (2004). *Machines who think* (2nd ed.). A. K. Peters. In recounting the 1956 Dartmouth Workshop, McCorduck explicitly credits John McCarthy as the originator of the term "artificial intelligence."

Schwab, K. (2016). The fourth industrial revolution: What it means, how to respond. World Economic Forum. https://www.weforum.org/stories/2016/01/the-fourth-industrial-revolution- what-it-means-and-how-to-respond/

CHAPTER 2

Pluralism as Architecture: The Philosophy of Multi-Agent Design

John Hines

Abstract This chapter develops a philosophical and technical framework for AI Pluralism—the design of AI systems as networks of diverse intelligences capable of sustaining multiple perspectives and negotiating toward provisional solutions. Drawing on John Dewey's democratic experimentalism, Donna Haraway's situated knowledges, and G.W.F. Hegel's dialectical method, we argue that when confronting morally complex and epistemically contested questions, truth emerges through structured interaction rather than monolithic optimization. We introduce FOAM (Framework for Openly Augmented Mediation), a computational architecture that operationalizes these philosophical insights through three core primitives: diverse agents with explicit stance vectors, deliberative protocols for structured critique, and sublation operators that weave contradictory perspectives into emergent syntheses. Using the fictional Port

This research was supported in part by National Science Foundation Small Business Innovation Research (NSF-SBIR) Grant No. 2431521. The views expressed are those of the author and do not necessarily reflect the views of the funding agency.

J. Hines (✉)
DebaterHub, Castro Valley, CA, USA

P. A. Rao (ed.), *AI Pluralism*,
https://doi.org/10.1007/978-3-032-06558-2_2

Aquilo climate council as a recurring example, we demonstrate how pluralistic AI can preserve productive disagreement while generating actionable outcomes. The chapter addresses key tensions in pluralistic design—richness versus clarity, memory versus revision, transparency versus privacy, and computational cost versus civic worth—arguing that these trade-offs are features, not bugs, of democratically legitimate AI systems.

Keywords AI Pluralism • Multi-agent systems • Epistemic diversity • Deliberative democracy • Situated knowledge • Dialectical AI • FOAM architecture • Democratic AI • Collective intelligence

2.1 Prelude: The Port Aquilo Climate Panel

Dawn clings to the glass façades of Port Aquilo's municipal hall as the city's climate-adaptation panel files into a horseshoe of walnut desks. Outside, tidal marshlands smoulder in a copper haze—beautiful, fragile, and destined for inundation within a generation unless the council finds a plan that balances ecological urgency with the livelihoods of shrimpers, insurers, and port-authority unions.

At the center of the chamber, a placid console hosts three language model agents. Their voices are distinct: ***Marè*** *speaks in the cadence of oceanographic journals,* ***Ceres*** *draws on anthropology and labor-rights archives, and* ***Aequitas*** *quotes budget ledgers and bond-market forecasts. Each has spent forty-eight hours ingesting the same data dossier, yet arrived at.*

contradictory recommendations. The panel's chair, Latoya Rivera, a former literature professor, addresses them not as tools but as witnesses. She invites rebuttals, forces clarifications, and occasionally turns to the public gallery where residents brandish placards announcing KEEP THE PORT ALIVE or LET THE MARSHES BREATHE.

By noon, a provisional decision emerges: a tiered sea-wall coupled with marsh-migration corridors and a compensation fund financed by shipping-levy futures. No single agent conceived the scheme; it coalesced in the friction among them and in dialogue with human testimony. As Rivera gavels the meeting closed, a reporter asks if the process wasn't dangerously inefficient.

She smiles: "Democracy is inefficient by design. Pluralistic AI just makes the inefficiency explicit—and negotiable."

We begin here because Port Aquilo's story, though fictional, stages the central claim of this chapter: **when questions are morally thick and epistemically messy, truth is an achievement of interaction, not a**

property discovered by solitary genius—human *or* machine. The vignette offers a touchstone to which we will return after mapping the conceptual terrain and issuing our closing provocations. While our Port Aquilo scenario is fictional, Goodnight (this volume) documents how actual cities from Singapore to Lagos are beginning to grapple with these challenges.

2.2 Why Pluralism, why Now?

The public conversation about artificial intelligence has swung between euphoria and dread. Modern language models can draft legal motions, diagnose rare diseases, and compose passable sonnets—yet they do so by collapsing the unruly diversity of their training data into a single, statistically average voice. That mechanical smoothing is convenient when you need a hotel recommendation. It becomes troubling when the same systems begin to moderate speech, adjudicate benefits, or mediate civic debate.

From a humanities perspective, this concern is not new. John Stuart Mill warned that societies which silence dissent substitute "a pallid unanimity for living truth" (Mill, 1859). John Dewey recast democracy itself as an experiment—one whose hypotheses must be aired in public, measured by consequences, and revised in the face of resistant facts (Dewey, 1927). For both thinkers, disagreement is not a design flaw but the oxygen that keeps collective intelligence alive.

The technical story leads to the same conclusion. Even scaling proponents acknowledge diminishing returns—Hoffmann et al. (2022) showed that Chinchilla (70B parameters) outperformed models 4x larger through better data efficiency. Meanwhile, Shumailov et al. (2024) proved that *model collapse* is inevitable when models train on synthetic data, producing increasingly homogenized outputs. Leading labs have pivoted accordingly: Anthropic's Constitutional AI (Bai et al., 2022) and OpenAI's safety-via-debate (Irving et al., 2018) employ multi-agent architectures precisely because, as Berkeley AI Research (2024) documented, **heterogeneity surfaces gaps that monoliths miss**.

Within AI research, the concept of "alignment" has evolved from simply stopping AI from doing harm to the more complex challenge of aligning systems with diverse human values. Traditional approaches often default to training one large model to produce acceptable behavior on average. But what is "acceptable," and to whom? These are not merely engineering puzzles; they are political, moral, and epistemic questions.

This recognition has led to growing interest in **Pluralistic Alignment**: approaches that preserve the full range of legitimate human disagreement rather than collapse it into a single voice. At the 2024 NeurIPS conference workshop on Pluralistic Alignment researchers (Sorensen et al., 2024) introduced three operational modes:

- **Overton pluralism**, which presents a spectrum of reasonable viewpoints within democratic discourse
- **Steerable pluralism**, which allows users to summon specific perspectives based on stated values
- **Distributional pluralism**, which calibrates outputs to reflect population-level diversity

While these modes provide a useful taxonomy, they are best understood not as interchangeable options but as **tensions to be held in productive friction**. Pluralism is not a design toggle but an **epistemic orientation**—a way of thinking about knowledge itself.

We call this orientation **AI Pluralism**: building systems composed not of a single voice, but of **networks of diverse intelligences** capable of sustaining perspectives, scrutinizing each other, and negotiating toward workable solutions. Port Aquilo's three agents model this approach in miniature—three voices, three constituencies, one provisional outcome emerging through productive contradiction.

A brief clarification: Pluralism is not relativism. Relativism holds that all claims are equally valid. Pluralism insists that **validity emerges through open contest among claims willing to give reasons**. Nor is pluralism satisfied by performative diversity. Its ambition is more demanding: to **build epistemic communities robust enough to host conflict without collapsing into nihilism**.

To understand how such communities might function, we turn now to three philosophical traditions that provide not just inspiration but architectural principles for pluralistic AI design.

2.3 Philosophical Foundations of Pluralism

Pluralism has technical modes, but it is not merely a technical construct. Its deepest roots lie in philosophical traditions that have long wrestled with the conditions under which knowledge emerges, thrives, and falters. If the NeurIPS workshop provides a **taxonomy of pluralism's**

operational forms, the philosophical canon offers **its justification**: why plurality matters—not as an engineering choice, but as a condition of flourishing thought and political life.

2.3.1 John Dewey: Democracy as Inquiry

In the early twentieth century, **John Dewey** redefined both **democracy** and **knowledge production** through the lens of **collective inquiry**. For Dewey, democracy is not simply a set of procedures or institutions, but a **method of problem-solving**—an ongoing experiment in which communities confront uncertainty together, propose hypotheses, and adjust course in light of stubborn facts.

His 1927 work, *The Public and Its Problems*, makes this plain. Dewey rejects the notion that truth resides solely in the mind of the expert or technocrat. Instead, **truth emerges from processes of communication, negotiation, and shared reflection**. Democracy, for Dewey, is thus epistemological at its core: it is the means by which societies test beliefs against experience and revise them in light of consequence.

The climate-adaptation panel in Port Aquilo exemplifies Dewey's experimental approach. When oceanographer Marè presents models predicting marsh inundation, these serve not as final verdicts but as hypotheses to be tested against local testimony. The panel doesn't simply accept these projections; it adjusts them based on historical patterns reported by longtime residents and alternative scenarios proposed by community advocates. This process mirrors Dewey's understanding of knowledge as emerging through communal testing rather than expert decree.

This framing resonates directly with the ambitions of **AI Pluralism**. In Dewey's schema, intelligence—whether human or machine—cannot be meaningfully aligned without **feedback from the community it serves**. The process of alignment is not one of **static optimization** but of **dynamic adjustment** through participatory inquiry. AI systems designed for pluralistic alignment should, in Dewey's terms, **engage in dialogue**, **receive critique**, and **adjust their inferences** as conditions change and as new perspectives enter the conversation.

Where the NeurIPS taxonomy offers modes of **representing multiple viewpoints**, Dewey urges us to recognize that pluralism is also a **methodology for collective sense-making**. In this frame, pluralism is not a choice between perspectives but a commitment to the **process by which perspectives meet and evolve**. Goodnight (this volume) extends this

Deweyan framework to the scale of cities, showing how urban epistemic communities embody democracy as inquiry in practice.

Dewey's vision of democracy as experimental inquiry finds its cognitive analog in contemporary neuroscience. Andy Clark's "predictive processing" framework (Clark, 2013) reveals that Dewey's political epistemology mirrors the brain's fundamental operations. Where Dewey.

describes democracy as hypothesis-testing in the social sphere, Clark shows the brain itself functioning as a prediction machine engaged in continuous experimentation.

Imagine the brain as a society of forecasters, each making predictions about what sensory information will arrive next. When reality differs from prediction—what neuroscientists call a "prediction error"—the brain must either revise its models or act to make the world conform to its expectations. This process resembles a miniature version of Dewey's democratic method: hypotheses encounter resistant facts, leading to revised understanding.

For AI Pluralism, this cognitive foundation suggests that Dewey's democratic experimentalism isn't merely a normative ideal but reflects how intelligence itself operates. Systems designed for pluralistic alignment should, like the predictive brain, engage multiple models simultaneously, receive error signals from diverse sources, and adjust inferences as conditions change. The error- signal negotiation that Clark identifies in neural circuitry becomes a design principle for pluralistic AI systems—embedding the mechanisms of Deweyan inquiry directly into their architecture.

2.3.2 Donna Haraway: Situated Knowledges

If **Dewey** provides the **method** of pluralism, **Donna Haraway** complicates the question of **who speaks**, **from where**, and **with what claims to authority**. In her landmark 1988 essay, *Situated Knowledges: The Science Question in Feminism and the Privilege of Partial Perspective*, Haraway challenges the prevailing myth of **objectivity**—the idea that knowledge can be produced from nowhere, by no one in particular (Haraway, 1988).

Instead, Haraway insists that all knowledge is **situated**—rooted in the **embodied experiences, social positions, and historical contexts** of its producers. This is not a declaration of relativism. Rather, it is a call to **accountability**: knowledge claims must be understood in relation to the positions from which they arise. Haraway rejects the "god trick"—the illusion of seeing everything from nowhere—and proposes **partial perspective** as a more honest, and ultimately more reliable, epistemic stance.

To understand situated knowledge, consider how different witnesses might describe a car accident. The truck driver's account, influenced by concerns about liability and professional standing, differs from the pedestrian's perspective, shaped by her position on the sidewalk and perhaps past experiences with traffic safety. Neither offers a complete "view from nowhere"— both are situated in particular bodies, histories, and interests. Yet together, these partial perspectives create a more robust understanding than either alone.

In Port Aquilo, the situated nature of knowledge becomes evident in how differently each AI agent frames the problem. Marè speaks from oceanographic journals, situating its analysis in scientific models that privilege measurable data about rising sea levels and marsh ecosystems.

Ceres, drawing on anthropology and labor rights archives, situates its perspective in the lived experiences of port workers and their communities. Neither agent claims a "view from nowhere"; each explicitly acknowledges its disciplinary positioning and the archives that inform its stance. This transparency about situatedness allows the panel to evaluate claims not as universal truths but as partial perspectives that, together, create a more robust understanding of the complex challenge.

For **AI Pluralism**, Haraway's intervention is transformative. The NeurIPS workshop's **distributional pluralism**—the calibration of outputs to reflect societal diversity—could be read as a statistical exercise: ensure that system outputs mirror demographic distributions. But **Haraway urges something deeper**. Distribution alone is not enough. We must also ask: **whose perspectives are being surfaced? Whose are erased? How do power, privilege, and marginalization shape the production of knowledge in AI systems?**

Haraway's framework reorients **pluralistic alignment** from a **surface-level representation of viewpoints** to a **critique of the epistemic structures** that shape which viewpoints count.

Situated knowledges challenge the very construction of **reasonableness** and **legitimacy** in Overton pluralism. What is deemed "within the bounds of acceptable discourse" is itself a **social artifact**, often excluding marginalized knowledges that defy normative frames.

For pluralistic AI systems, this demands a **reassessment of training data, model architectures, and evaluation benchmarks**. It is not enough to ensure that outputs are balanced across demographic lines. Systems must be designed to **surface and sustain epistemically marginalized perspectives**—even when these challenge the system's own embedded assumptions.

Haraway's rejection of the "god trick" and insistence on situated knowledge finds profound embodiment in one of history's oldest continuous learning traditions. Chavrusa—paired study of Talmud—has been the cornerstone of Jewish intellectual practice for millennia, institutionalizing the very accountability to position that Haraway advocates.

In chavrusa practice, students dissect texts through iterative challenge: one reads a passage aloud, the other probes its logical and ethical coherence, prompting dialectical twists. Mastery emerges not from rote memorization but from the capacity to pivot positions, formulate counter- interpretations, and anticipate objections—a direct manifestation of situated knowledge. Students must be explicit about their interpretive standpoints, saying "I find this ambiguous because..." rather than simply asserting "This means..." This practice of positioning oneself in relation to the text mirrors Haraway's call for accountability to perspective.

For AI Pluralism, Haraway's theoretical framework thus finds validation in traditions that predates modern theory by millennia. What she formulates as feminist epistemology, chavrusa has practiced as pedagogy. This convergence suggests that situated knowledge is not merely a.

corrective to Western science's pretensions of neutrality, but a recurring solution to the fundamental challenge of robust knowledge production—one that pluralistic AI systems must incorporate through stance vectors, position-switching, and explicit accountability to the conditions under which perspectives arise.

2.3.3 G.W.F. Hegel: Dialectic and Sublation

If **Dewey** offers the **methodological framework** for pluralism as inquiry, and **Haraway** demands **accountability to situated perspective**, **G.W.F. Hegel** provides the **epistemic mechanics** for how **disagreement itself can generate new knowledge**. In **Hegel's dialectic**, contradictions are not merely obstacles to be resolved; they are **the motor of intellectual and social progress** (Hegel, 1807).

Central to Hegel's system is the process of **sublation** (*Aufhebung*), a term that resists easy translation. **Sublation** is at once **negation, preservation, and elevation**: the simultaneous holding of oppositions in tension and their transformation into a **higher-order synthesis**— though "synthesis" is too flat a word for the dynamic layering that **sublation** implies. It is a process in which opposing concepts, perspectives, or historical forces **interact, conflict, and eventually yield to a new configuration** that **carries forward elements of both, but transcends neither entirely**.

Hegel's dialectic offers more than a simple formula of thesis-antithesis-synthesis; it provides a way of thinking about how meaningful progress emerges precisely through contradiction rather than despite it. For Hegel, truth is not a static entity but a process—it develops through the very tensions that seem to undermine it.

Take a contemporary example: the tension between privacy and security in digital systems. A simplistic approach might try to maximize one at the expense of the other, or seek a weak compromise that satisfies neither concern. Hegelian sublation, by contrast, doesn't resolve this tension but elevates it. A sublated approach to privacy and security recognizes their interdependence: without meaningful privacy protections, security measures lose public trust and therefore effectiveness; without robust security frameworks, privacy becomes impossible to maintain. The resulting system preserves both values not by averaging them but by transforming how we understand their relationship—creating security through privacy rather than against it.

The Port Aquilo resolution exemplifies Hegelian sublation in action. Initially, the three AI agents present seemingly incompatible recommendations: Marè argues for abandoning the port to create migration corridors for marsh ecosystems; Ceres advocates maintaining port infrastructure to protect livelihoods; and Aequitas proposes a market-based solution using shipping-levy futures. Rather than selecting one approach or averaging them into a weak compromise, the panel's deliberations produce something new: a tiered sea-wall that simultaneously protects critical infrastructure, creates marsh-migration corridors in strategic locations, and establishes a compensation fund financed by shipping-levy futures. This solution doesn't eliminate the tensions between ecological, social, and economic priorities; it elevates them into a new configuration that preserves each concern while transforming how they relate to one another.

For **AI Pluralism**, Hegel's dialectic offers something crucial: a **framework for working through disagreement** when **deliberation alone stalls**. Pluralistic systems must therefore be capable not only of **sustaining multiple perspectives**, nor merely of **deliberating among them**, but of **metabolizing their contradictions into emergent forms of knowledge**.

This is not a passive process. **Sublation demands active engagement with contradiction**—a **confrontation with difference** that transforms both sides, yielding **something new** without erasing the memory of what came before. **Pluralistic AI architectures**, if they are to truly embody this dialectical dynamic, must be designed to **hold tension long enough for emergent resolutions to arise**—even if those resolutions are **temporary, contingent, and open to future revision**.

For AI Pluralism, this insight is revolutionary. It suggests that the goal is not to eliminate disagreement by finding a lowest common denominator, but to create systems that can hold contradictions long enough for new possibilities to emerge. When pluralistic architectures.

process conflicting agent outputs, they shouldn't simply vote or average; they ought identify patterns of complementarity beneath apparent opposition. The result isn't compromise but emergence—new configurations that couldn't have been predicted by any single agent working alone.

Hegelian dialectic, in this sense, provides the **epistemic underpinning for the dynamic architectures of AI Pluralism**. Systems designed to embody pluralism must be capable not only of **presenting diverse viewpoints**, not only of **deliberating toward consensus**, but of **holding contradiction as a generative force**—**sublating** rather than **resolving** disagreement.

2.3.4 Pluralism as Epistemic Community

These three philosophers and their cognitive/cultural manifestations furnish an integrated conceptual infrastructure for AI Pluralism. Dewey demonstrates that intelligence itself functions through experimental feedback and continuous adjustment. Haraway shows that knowledge must acknowledge its situatedness to achieve robust objectivity. And Hegel's dialectic provides the dynamic engine through which contradictions generate movement toward emergent configurations.

Together, they suggest that pluralism is not a static design choice but a living epistemic community—one that operates at every scale from neural circuitry to cultural institution. This community thrives on contested inquiry, situated accountability, and dialectical emergence.

Remove any dimension, and the community collapses into dogmatism, nihilism, or epistemic stagnation.

Imagine this community as a complex forest rather than a monoculture plantation. In a forest, diverse species occupy different niches, compete for resources, and yet ultimately sustain one another through their very differences. Similarly, pluralistic knowledge systems require diversity not as an aesthetic choice but as a functional necessity—different perspectives create resilience against error and adaptation to changing conditions. Just as forest health depends on maintaining tension between competing species, epistemic health requires preserving productive contradiction between situated viewpoints. Goodnight's analysis (this volume) of epistemic communities operating at multiple scales—from global networks to local "foam"—demonstrates how this community functions in urban contexts.

This remarkable convergence across philosophical tradition, cognitive science, and cultural practice reveals pluralism not as a modern innovation but as a recurring solution to the fundamental challenge of collective intelligence. What these diverse domains share is the insight that knowledge improves when rival interpretations are obliged to justify themselves in dialogue—when diverse perspectives engage in structured contestation that preserves tension long enough for new configurations to emerge.

Returning to Port Aquilo's climate-adaptation panel, we can now recognize how the council's decision-making process enacts this epistemic community. The three AI agents—Marè, Ceres, and Aequitas—embody Haraway's situated perspectives; their interactions with human testimony exemplify Dewey's experimental inquiry; and their eventual sublation into a provisional sea-wall plan manifests Hegel's dialectical progression. What appeared as a pragmatic civic process now reveals itself as philosophy-in-action.

This integrated foundation prepares us to move from pluralism as concept to pluralism as architecture—to translate these philosophical, cognitive, and cultural insights into the concrete design of FOAM. Section 2.4 will show how FOAM braids these mechanisms into a programmable substrate that both honors human traditions and advances AI research, creating a framework where multiple agents, situated knowledge, and deliberative protocols interact to generate emergent, provisional alignments.

2.4 FOAM — Framework for Openly Augmented Mediation

The philosophical foundations established in Section 2.3 provide not merely conceptual inspiration but a design blueprint for AI Pluralism. To bridge theory and practice, we draw on Peter Sloterdijk's spatial metaphor of "foam" from his *Spheres* trilogy (Sloterdijk, 2016). Unlike traditional Western metaphysics that often seeks unity, singularity, and monolithic foundations, Sloterdijk offers us foam as a post-metaphysical image of plurality—a structure where no single bubble can claim to be the origin or center of the whole.

Sloterdijk's foam concept operates as a spatial counterpart to our philosophical triad. Where Dewey's experimentalism requires multiple hypotheses to test against experience, Sloterdijk's foam provides a structural image of these hypotheses as coexisting bubbles—each maintaining internal coherence while remaining vulnerable to external pressure. Where Haraway rejects the "god trick" of seeing from nowhere, Sloterdijk's bubbles are inherently situated—each offering a view from somewhere specific, with its own atmosphere and internal logic. And where Hegel's dialectic requires the preservation of contradiction within a higher synthesis, Sloterdijk's foam bubbles neither merge into uniformity nor remain in isolation—they touch, deform, and sustain one another in what he calls "co-fragile" relationships.

This co-fragility is crucial for understanding FOAM's design ethos. In Sloterdijk's foam, bubbles derive their resilience not from rigid boundaries but from mutual support—what he terms "connected isolations" or "co-isolated associations." The architectural principle here transcends mere coexistence; it suggests that distinct perspectives gain strength precisely through their adjacency to difference. Just as foam bubbles share walls without collapsing into one another, FOAM's AI agents maintain their epistemological distinctness while allowing their boundaries to be reshaped through encounter.

FOAM (*Framework for Openly Augmented Mediation*) extends this metaphor into computational space. The name fuses Sloterdijk's foam with Hegelian sublation—creating a system where distinct bubbles of perspective interact, challenge one another, and generate emergent configurations that preserve rather than erase their differences. Each component of FOAM deliberately operationalizes a philosophical insight: Dewey's experimental inquiry becomes its iterative feedback loops; Haraway's situated knowledge manifests in its stance vectors; and Hegel's dialectic drives its sublation operators.

2.4.1 *Why we Need Programmable Pluralism*

At its core, FOAM is a response to a **civic design problem**: how do we build digital interlocutors that reflect democratic complexity rather than flatten it? Traditional AI pipelines enforce a **single dominant narrative** by collapsing diversity into an average. FOAM rejects that monolith.

Instead, it treats each agent as an **epistemic bubble**—a voice with its own historical archives, normative assumptions, and reasoning style—anchored in a **stance vector** that encodes domain role (e.g. economist, ethicist), value commitments, and preferred argument schema.

FOAM doesn't simply implement technical solutions; it embodies the philosophical principles explored earlier. Each element of its architecture corresponds to a specific philosophical insight: diverse agents embody Haraway's situated knowledge, deliberative protocols operationalize Dewey's experimental inquiry, and sublation operators manifest Hegel's dialectical process.

These aren't mere metaphors but design principles that shape how the system functions at every level.

Philosophically, FOAM operationalizes Dewey's **inquiry**, Haraway's **situatedness**, and Hegel's **sublation** by embedding **feedback loops** and **contestable claims** at every layer. Technically, it draws on cognitive science principles of modularity and error-signal negotiation: bubbles generate hypotheses, cross-examine rivals, and converge only as far as provisional consensus allows. This design extends beyond metaphor: FOAM's **mediation graph** archives every utterance and objection, enabling users to trace not only **what** was decided but **how** and **why** deliberation unfolded.

Imagine a mediation graph as a detailed transcript that doesn't just record what was said but also maps how ideas influenced each other. A mediation graph captures the entire deliberative process—which agent proposed which idea, which objections were raised, how proposals were revised in response to critique, and which threads of thought eventually contributed to the final outcome. Like a journal of congressional proceedings, it serves both as historical record and as a tool for understanding how consensus emerged or where disagreements remain.

Nearly every civic institution—from courts to legislatures—relies on recorded debates to maintain legitimacy. FOAM brings that archival imperative to AI systems, turning each inference into a **traceable artifact** of collective intelligence rather than a black-box verdict. Goodnight's analysis (this volume) of how cities navigate AI adoption illustrates why programmable pluralism matters: urban communities face precisely the kinds of "morally thick and epistemically messy" challenges that resist singular optimization.

2.4.2 *The Three Core Primitives of FOAM*

FOAM represents not a static architecture but an evolving framework. The system we describe here represents its current implementation, but its design allows for progressive enhancement as new capabilities emerge. This evolutionary approach reflects Dewey's understanding of democracy as continuous experimental adjustment, with each iteration improving upon previous implementations based on practical experience and emerging capabilities.

FOAM's architecture rests on three interlocking primitives, each deeply rooted in both human tradition and modern computation:

1. **Diverse Agents**—Each agent embodies a **distinct standpoint**, implemented via prompt-engineered personas or adapter-chained modules. These standpoints can be disciplinary (legal, anthropological), normative (utilitarian, rights-based), or cultural (Indigenous, minority). Their heterogeneity ensures that the system never retreats to monotony.

   This primitive operationalizes Haraway's situated knowledge and Dewey's experimental method. Like chavrusa partners who must justify their readings with specific textual anchors, FOAM agents declare their epistemic positioning explicitly. This transparency transforms what might otherwise be mere performative diversity into accountability—a direct response to Haraway's.

   call for positioned responsibility. Following cognitive science insights about the value of specialized modules, these agents are not generalists but experts in particular domains, bringing depth rather than breadth to the deliberative community.

   To understand the role of diverse agents in practice, consider how Port Aquilo's climate panel might approach a specific question about marsh preservation timeframes. Marè might draw on oceanographic models that predict sea-level rise rates, citing specific data sets and simulation methodologies. Ceres might counter by examining how Indigenous communities have managed similar coastlines for centuries, drawing on anthropological archives and oral histories. And Aequitas might analyze the economic feasibility of various adaptation timelines, citing bond market projections and infrastructure depreciation schedules. Each agent not only offers a different answer but approaches the question through a different epistemic framework altogether.

2. **Deliberative Protocols**—Drawing on multi-turn debate training, agents engage through **critique exchanges** and **evidence-citing threads**, guided by inference-time scaffolding. Rather than pooling outputs blindly, they **cross-examine**: objection tags ("missing data," "value conflict," "logical gap") trigger targeted rebuttals, mirroring Talmudic chavrusa and cultural deliberation practices.

   These protocols embody Dewey's experimental method and Haraway's situated accountability. Just as traditional deliberative practices institutionalize speaker rotation and active listening, FOAM's critique exchange ensures that each perspective receives both voice and scrutiny. The structured objection tags create what cognitive scientists would recognize as prediction-error signals—forcing revision when claims fail to match evidence. This mechanism transforms mere opinion exchange into the reason-giving dialogue that produces legitimate coordination.

   Another useful visualization is to picture the mediation process as a river delta rather than a linear stream. Multiple channels of thought diverge, intersect, and occasionally reunite, all flowing toward a common destination. Some channels carry more volume than others, but even smaller tributaries shape the overall landscape. This delta image captures how FOAM processes multiple strands of reasoning in parallel, allowing them to influence one another without forcing them into a single channel.

3. **Sublation Operators**—Inspired by Hegel, FOAM never forces a single winner. Instead, **sublation modules** weave agent drafts into **composite proposals**, preserving minority reports as footnotes. A **jury meta-agent** scores each draft for **coherence**, **novelty**, and **civic impact**, supplying **gradient weights** that inform revision. This loop runs until marginal improvements fall below a threshold, then yields a **provisional synthesis** alongside a **dissent memo**.

   A sublation operator functions like a skilled moderator who identifies complementary elements in seemingly opposed positions. Rather than forcing agreement, the sublation operator weaves together threads from different perspectives, preserving important tensions while creating a.

   coherent whole. It doesn't just identify overlap; it actively constructs new configurations that honor the distinctive contributions of each perspective while transforming them into something that transcends their individual limitations.

Here, Hegel's dialectical process—where contradiction generates movement toward higher-order configurations—finds technical expression. The Port Aquilo vignette that opened our chapter demonstrates sublation in action: the tiered sea-wall coupled with marsh-migration corridors emerged not from a single agent's vision but from the productive tension among competing perspectives. FOAM's sublation operators institutionalize this pattern, treating disagreement not as noise to be filtered but as the very signal from which new configurations emerge.

Together, these primitives form a **Mediation Loop** whose moving parts can be tuned by context: more agents for high-stakes situations, fewer for rapid prototyping; wider dissent budgets for policy debates, and tighter windows for time-sensitive advisories.

2.4.3 Conceptual Mapping: From Philosophy to Architecture

AI Pluralism's philosophical commitments acquire concrete form within the FOAM architecture. The table below highlights how its core components operationalize key concepts introduced earlier, translating epistemic principles into system functions. FOAM's design thus extends AI Pluralism beyond metaphor. Each philosophical term becomes a programmable primitive—turning rhetorical and epistemological commitments into architectural mechanisms for coordination, accountability, and synthesis.

Philosophical concept	*FOAM architectural expression*	*Operational function*
Sublation (Aufhebung)	*Sublation operator*	Performs structured synthesis with traceable dissent, integrating divergent agent outputs into provisional consensus while preserving minority positions.
Situated knowledge	*Stance vector*	Encodes each agent's epistemic position—Its domain role, values, and reasoning schema—Enabling context-aware inference and accountability.
Dialectical deliberation	*Mediation graph*	Records the topology of agent interactions and objections, creating a deliberation pipeline that makes reasoning pathways visible and auditable.

2.4.4 The FOAM Mediation Loop in Action

The FOAM Mediation Loop balances structured process with adaptive flexibility. While the steps proceed in a defined sequence, the system allows for variation in timing, depth, and emphasis depending on the context. This balance reflects the philosophical insight that vitality emerges not from rigid conformity but from the dynamic tension between structure and freedom.

1. **Seeding.** A **Dialogue Manager** instantiates *n* agents, each tagged with a stance vector that declares role, values, and reasoning template. Metadata records provenance and training sources.
2. **Local Drafting.** Agents independently craft initial responses, grounding claims via **Cache-Augmented Generation** or retrieval from curated corpora. Each response is accompanied by **source citations** and a confidence estimate. Cache-Augmented Generation allows an AI to access a specialized reference library while it works. Rather than relying solely on general knowledge baked into its training, the system can consult specific texts, data sets, or records to ground its reasoning in particular sources.
3. **Cross-Examination.** Drafts circulate; agents emit **objections** with structured tags (e.g. 'ethical blind spot'). Objections become first-class nodes in the mediation graph, not mere marginalia.
4. **Jury Deliberation.** A **meta-agent cluster**—trained on multi-perspective evaluation procedures—scores each draft-objection pair. Scores translate into **feedback gradients**, highlighting claims requiring reinforcement or retraction.
5. **Revision & Sublation.** Agents absorb gradients and produce revised drafts. A **sublation operator** aggregates overlapping contributions into a **composite proposal**, ensuring that surviving tokens preserve traces of contested threads.

Outcome Emission. The system emits: (a) the composite proposal, (b) a **linked bibliography**, (c) a **dissent report**, and (d) the **mediation graph** for dashboard visualization. This loop directly instantiates the philosophical principles explored in Sect. 2.3. The seeding phase implements Haraway's accountability to position through explicit stance vectors. Local drafting mirrors cognitive modularity. Cross-examination operationalizes Dewey's insistence that hypotheses require testing against resistant facts. Jury deliberation enacts the deliberative protocols found in diverse cultural traditions, where proposals must withstand scrutiny. Revision and sublation embody Hegel's dialectical progression, where contradictions generate movement toward higher-order configurations that preserve rather than erase tension. And outcome emission ensures the transparency that identifies as the foundation of legitimate coordination.

To illustrate this process in action, let's return to Port Aquilo. In drafting the climate adaptation plan, Marè initially argues for complete marsh restoration, citing oceanographic models that predict catastrophic flooding without natural buffers. During cross-examination, Ceres objects with the tag 'ethical blind spot,' noting that this approach ignores displacement of port workers. The jury meta-agent assigns this objection high weight, forcing Marè to revise its proposal to acknowledge livelihood impacts. Meanwhile, Aequitas proposes market-based incentives for ecological protection, which Marè challenges as insufficient given timeframe constraints.t.

Through multiple iterations, the sublation operator identifies complementary elements across all drafts: Marè's ecological urgency, Ceres's concern for workers, and Aequitas's financing mechanism. The eventual composite proposal—a tiered sea-wall with migration corridors and compensation fund—preserves each agent's core concern while transforming them into a configuration that none independently proposed.

Each cycle is either time-boxed or stops when improvement reaches pre-established limit thresholds, echoing democratic deadlines. The loop itself is the artifact of pluralistic alignment, not merely the final output.

2.4.5 *Ethical and Governance Considerations*

The ethical considerations in FOAM implementation reflect the very dialectical process the system embodies. Just as Hegel recognized that contradictions drive progress when properly held, FOAM's governance approach acknowledges tensions between transparency and privacy, diversity and responsibility, computational efficiency and deliberative depth. Rather than attempting to eliminate these tensions, FOAM's governance approach aims to hold them in productive balance, allowing each to inform and enhance the other.

FOAM's transparency and modularity open both **possibilities** and **risks**:

- **Accountability.** Mediation graphs tie claims to stance vectors, enabling post hoc audits of **responsibility**—who said what, when, and why.
- **Power asymmetries.** Even with multiple agents, minority voices can be drowned if their metadata lacks visibility. This requires **real-time minority shout alerts** and **dashboard equity metrics** to ensure all perspectives receive adequate consideration.
- **Privacy.** When FOAM ingests user data—student prompts, proprietary corpora— decisions about what to log publicly versus what to redact become governance questions, not mere code flags.
- **Resource justice.** Computational bursts for multi-agent loops impose environmental costs. Institutions must weigh FOAM's benefits against carbon budgets, echoing broader debates on sustainable AI.

These considerations directly engage the philosophical tensions we've explored. The accountability mechanisms respond to Haraway's call for responsible positioning and Dewey's emphasis on consequences. The concern with power asymmetries acknowledges the risk that even in pluralistic systems, marginalized voices can be silenced. The privacy questions echo traditional deliberative practices' careful balance between openness and discretion, where certain sensitive matters might be discussed with controlled audience. And the resource justice consideration extends pluralistic values to include environmental impacts, recognizing that **AI Pluralism**'s computational costs must be justified by its civic benefits.

As we move into Sect. 2.5 exploration of tensions and trade-offs, we carry forward this integrated understanding of FOAM as not merely a software architecture but a sociotechnical system—one that encodes in silicon the philosophical insights and cultural wisdom that have sustained pluralistic knowledge-making across diverse traditions and contexts.

2.5 Tensions and Trade-Offs in Pluralistic AI

Pluralism promises richer insight and greater legitimacy, but it also brings **inevitable frictions**. These trade-offs have deep historical precedents and bear directly on how—and whether—we choose to deploy pluralistic architectures. Below we unpack four core tensions, each illustrated with evocative analogies and practical considerations.

2.5.1 Richness Vs. Clarity

When Diderot and d'Alembert assembled the first *Encyclopèdie*, critics warned that including every conceivable viewpoint would overwhelm readers. Too many marginal voices might obscure the central narrative—or so the censors feared. Yet Enlightenment editors resisted, believing that intellectual vitality required **plural testimony**, even at the cost of reader fatigue.

This tension between richness and clarity manifests daily in Port Aquilo's climate council. When local fishers present testimony alongside oceanographers, when Indigenous knowledge keepers share observations that sometimes contradict scientific models, the resulting picture becomes both richer and more complex. While a single authoritative voice might offer comforting clarity, it would miss the textured understanding that emerges from multiple perspectives. The central challenge becomes not eliminating complexity but making it navigable.

The design challenge is to strike an editorial balance—much like a museum curator arranging diverse artifacts so that the installation feels coherent but never monolithic. Tuning the "dissent budget" (how many voices to surface at once) and offering cognitive scaffolds (visual timelines, thematic tags) become critical levers. As with any curated collection, some depth must be held in reserve for specialist explorers, while the main floor guides general visitors through a clear narrative.

For pluralistic AI systems, this means designing interfaces that don't overwhelm users with all possible perspectives simultaneously. FOAM addresses this through "progressive disclosure"— showing a synthesized view initially, with options to explore dissenting positions and underlying reasoning for those who want to dig deeper. This approach honors both clarity and richness by recognizing that different users have different information needs at different moments.

2.5.2 Memory Vs. Revision

Constitutions embody societies' founding principles, yet nearly every democratic polity includes amendment procedures, acknowledging that **no charter can foresee every future challenge**.

The U.S. Constitution, for example, has been amended 27 times in over two centuries—even as its original text remains a hallowed artifact. This duality—**stability through memory, flexibility through revision**—defines enduring governance.

In Port Aquilo, this tension emerges when historical flood patterns documented by long-time residents seem to contradict new climate models. Should the council privilege local memory or scientific revision? The wisest approach recognizes both: memory provides continuity and cultural grounding, while revision enables adaptation to changing conditions. The question isn't which to choose but how to honor both simultaneously.

FOAM adopts the same posture: every agent utterance, objection, and synthesis is immutably logged, while the system also supports **forking** and **versioning**. When new data or ethical frameworks emerge, past decisions need not be erased but can be **contextualized**, producing a transparent lineage of how collective judgments evolved. Users thus gain both the reassurance of an audit trail and the freedom to update their stance when circumstances change.

Yet this archival richness carries a practical cost: storage demands, interface complexity, and the risk that users defer action pending endless reconsideration. FOAM addresses this by.

time-boxing deliberations and embedding **"sunset clauses"** for provisional syntheses—reminders that any resolution is subject to future amendment. Just as a legislature enshrines a one-year review of new laws, pluralistic systems can embed similar institutionalized checkpoints.

2.5.3 Transparency Vs. Privacy

Eighteenth-century Parisian salons were renowned forums for literary and political debate—but only because patrons felt safe to speak freely behind closed doors. Publishing every witticism or misstep would have silenced the very candor that made salons vital. The French called this the *salon paradox*: **openness and discretion must coexist**.

In Port Aquilo, some stakeholders might hesitate to share sensitive information—perhaps about vulnerable infrastructure or insurance risks—if every word becomes public record. Yet without transparency, the process loses legitimacy in the eyes of the community. The council must therefore create zones of appropriate disclosure: perhaps recording general discussion while protecting specific vulnerabilities, or anonymizing certain contributions while maintaining their substance.

FOAM's mediation graphs promise radical transparency—every node and edge exposed for audit. However, in civic contexts, participants may reveal sensitive personal experiences or commercial secrets. Releasing raw transcripts in full could chill participation or risk privacy breaches. The solution lies in **selective redaction** and **tiered access**: sensitive nodes can be anonymized or sealed, while general audience views still convey the structure of dissent and support.

Deciding which layers to publish is less a technical problem than a **governance question**.

Who—developers, community stewards, independent ombudspersons—should arbitrate.

privacy-vs-transparency trade-offs? As with judicial in camera sessions, FOAM deployments may need advisory boards empowered to sanction disclosures and protect vulnerable actors. The goal is not secrecy but **responsible openness**.

2.5.4 Cost Vs. Worth

Gothic cathedrals required multigenerational labor and vast stone quarries—but communities deemed the civic and spiritual return worth the outlay. Here, the **worth** was not measured in economic terms alone but in shared identity and awe. Pluralistic AI systems likewise demand more computational energy, longer run-times, and greater human facilitation than monolithic models.

Port Aquilo's council process involves substantial resources: staff time to prepare briefings, community energy for public hearings, technological infrastructure to support deliberation.

Would a simple executive decision be more efficient? Perhaps—but efficiency isn't the only value at stake. The deliberative process creates not just decisions but public understanding, relationship-building across difference, and legitimacy that reduces implementation friction.

Institutions must weigh: is the benefit of richer deliberation, improved legitimacy, and deeper learning enough to justify higher cloud bills and carbon footprints? FOAM's **adaptive agent pools** help: routine queries trigger only a couple of lightweight personas, while complex debates unlock the full polyphony. Ultimately, just as cathedral builders petitioned congregations to fund construction, FOAM advocates must make a **civic**

case for pluralism's value. In fields like health policy or climate adaptation—where errors cost lives—the case is easier. For low-stakes domains, scaled-down deployments or hybrid models may strike a more sustainable balance.

Recognizing that cost is not a bug but a feature keeps us honest about pluralism's true price.

2.5.5 Addressing Common Criticisms of Pluralistic AI

As with any architectural innovation, pluralistic AI faces skepticism. We address three common critiques not as dismissals but as generative tensions that sharpen design.

Efficiency and Computational Costs

Critics rightfully question whether pluralistic systems justify their computational expense. Running multiple agents in parallel demands more processing power, memory, and energy than single-model approaches. This is not merely an economic concern but an environmental and accessibility issue—high computation costs could limit pluralistic AI to wealthy institutions, reinforcing existing power imbalances.

FOAM addresses this through tiered deployment strategies. Not every query requires the full ensemble—many can be handled by smaller agent cohorts or even single agents for routine tasks. The system implements computational gradient descent: it starts with minimal agent activation and scales up only when complexity thresholds are crossed.

The most compelling response to efficiency criticisms, however, isn't technical but normative. Democracy has never optimized for efficiency—it optimizes for legitimacy, representation, and error-correction over time. Pluralistic AI makes a similar tradeoff, investing computational resources to gain epistemic robustness and deliberative legitimacy. The question becomes not whether pluralistic systems are more expensive—they often are—but whether what they purchase is worth the price.

Time-Sensitive Decision Making

A second critique concerns speed: can pluralistic systems respond quickly enough in crisis scenarios? When a hospital needs immediate medical guidance or when disaster response.

requires split-second coordination, the deliberative loops of FOAM might seem luxuriously slow.

Here, we distinguish between three time horizons. For truly immediate responses (seconds to minutes), FOAM can operate in "emergency mode," where pre-trained agent ensembles with specialized crisis protocols deliver rapid assessments with explicit uncertainty markers. For intermediate horizons (hours to days), FOAM implements parallel rather than serial deliberation, with time-boxed contributions and forced-choice resolution mechanisms. And for longer horizons (weeks to years), full pluralistic deliberation remains optimal.

Importantly, even time-pressured decisions benefit from pluralistic foundations. A single-agent emergency response grounded in prior pluralistic deliberation will be more robust than one trained only on consensus data. The key is modularity—designing systems where agents can operate independently when necessary but retain the diverse epistemologies that make pluralism valuable.

Echo Chambers and Selection Bias

Perhaps the most subtle criticism asks whether pluralistic AI simply replicates human biases in agent selection. If developers choose which perspectives to include, doesn't this merely shift the power of curation from model training to agent selection? What prevents pluralistic systems from becoming sophisticated echo chambers that give the appearance of diversity while actually reinforcing dominant viewpoints?

This concern cuts to the heart of FOAM's governance model. Three mechanisms provide partial answers. First, stance vectors are explicit and public, making selection biases visible rather than hidden. Second, FOAM incorporates "perspective discovery" processes that proactively identify missing viewpoints through gap analysis in the deliberative space. Third, the self-reflexive agent described in our thought experiments (Sect. 5.6) serves as a continuous audit mechanism, flagging when the system's perspective diversity narrows.

Most importantly, FOAM shifts the focus from selecting "correct" perspectives to ensuring procedural fairness in how perspectives interact. By making the rules of deliberation explicit and contestable, the system allows for the ongoing correction of perspective imbalances. The goal is not perfect initial representation—an impossible standard—but a self-correcting system that improves representation over time through transparency and ongoing critique.

These responses do not eliminate the tensions inherent in pluralistic AI. Rather, they transform criticisms from fatal flaws into design challenges—productive frictions that drive the ongoing evolution of more robust, fair, and practical pluralistic architectures.

Acknowledgments This research was supported in part by National Science Foundation Small Business Innovation Research (NSF-SBIR) Grant No. 2431521 and by a grant from Cosmos Ventures. The views expressed are those of the author and do not necessarily reflect the views of the funding agencies.

References

Bai, Y., Kadavath, S., Kundu, S., Askell, A., Kernion, J., Jones, A., Chen, A., Goldie, A., Mirhoseini, A., McKinnon, C., Chen, C., Olsson, C., Olah, C., Hernandez, D., Drain, D., Ganguli, D., Li, D., Tran-Johnson, E., Perez, E., … Kaplan, J. (2022). *Constitutional AI: Harmlessness from AI feedback* (arXiv:2212.08073). arXiv. https://doi.org/10.48550/arXiv.2212.08073.

Berkeley AI Research. (2024, February 18). *The shift from models to compound AI systems.* The Berkeley Artificial Intelligence Research Blog. https://bair.berkeley.edu/blog/2024/02/18/compound-ai-systems/

Clark, A. (2013). *Surfing uncertainty: Prediction, action, and the embodied mind.* Oxford University Press.

Dewey, J. (1927). *The public and its problems.* Henry Holt and Company.

Haraway, D. J. (1988). Situated knowledges: The science question in feminism and the privilege of partial perspective. *Feminist Studies, 14*(3), 575–599.

Hegel, G. W. F. (1807). *Phenomenology of spirit* (A. V. Miller, Trans.). Oxford University Press. (Original work published 1807).

Hoffmann, J., Borgeaud, S., Mensch, A., Buchatskaya, E., Cai, T., Rutherford, E., Casas, D. de. L., Hendricks, L. A., Welbl, J., Clark, A., Hennigan, T., Noland, E., Millican, K., Driessche, G. v. d., Damoc, B., Guy, A., Osindero, S., Simonyan, K., Rae, J. W., … Sifre, L. (2022). *Training compute-optimal large language models* (arXiv:2203.15556). arXiv. https://doi.org/10.48550/arXiv.2203.15556.

Irving, G., Christiano, P., & Amodei, D. (2018). *AI safety via debate* (arXiv:1805.00899). arXiv. https://doi.org/10.48550/arXiv.1805.00899.

Mill, J. S. (1859). *On liberty.* John W. Parker and Son.

Shumailov, I., Shumaylov, Z., Zhao, Y., Papernot, N., Anderson, R., & Gal, Y. (2024). AI models collapse when trained on recursively generated data. *Nature, 631*(8022), 755–759. https://doi.org/10.1038/s41586-024-07566-y

Sloterdijk, P. (2016). *Foams: Spheres volume III: Plural spherology* (W. Hoban, Trans.). Semiotext(e). (Original work published 2004).

Sorensen, T., Jiang, L., Hwang, J. D., Levine, S., Pyatkin, V., West, P., … Choi, Y..(2024). Value kaleidoscope: Engaging AI with pluralistic human values, rights, and duties. In *Proceedings of the AAAI Conference on Artificial Intelligence, 38*(18), 19937–19947.

CHAPTER 3

Enhancing Explainability and Contestability through AI Pluralism and Rhetorical Argumentation

P. Anand Rao

Abstract This chapter argues that AI pluralism, the deliberate differentiation of AI agents to enable multiple situated perspectives in deliberation, provides a crucial link between technical interpretability and democratic accountability in artificial intelligence systems. As AI increasingly influences high-stakes domains such as healthcare, finance, and criminal justice, the dual challenges of explainability (making AI decisions transparent and understandable) and contestability (enabling meaningful challenge and revision) become paramount.

Keywords AI pluralism • Explainability • Contestability • Multi-Agent Language Systems (MALS) • Rhetorical Argumentation • Computational argumentation • Deliberative protocols • Situated knowledge • Debate-centered systems • Constitutional AI

Drawing on the philosophical foundations outlined in Chap. 2, which include Dewey's pragmatism, Hegel's dialectical method, and Haraway's

P. A. Rao (✉)
University of Mary Washington, Fredericksburg, VA, USA
e-mail: arao@umw.edu

P. A. Rao (ed.), *AI Pluralism*,
https://doi.org/10.1007/978-3-032-06558-2_3

situated knowledges, the chapter demonstrates how Multi-Agent Language Systems (MALS) can implement AI pluralism through rhetorical argumentation frameworks. Unlike traditional post-hoc explanations that may disconnect from actual decision processes, pluralistic systems create authentic dialogical spaces where diverse AI agents engage in structured debate, making both their reasoning and value assumptions transparent.

The chapter presents concrete implementation strategies and references case studies from FairPlay, Constitutional AI, and community-centered governance models. By treating AI decisions as provisional hypotheses open to ongoing challenge, this approach fosters more transparent, accountable, and ethically aligned artificial intelligence systems.

3.1 Introduction

Building on the FOAM architecture and its philosophical foundations presented in Chap. 2, this chapter demonstrates how the three core primitives—differentiated agents, deliberative protocols, and sublation operators—translate directly into concrete tools for addressing AI's dual accountability crisis. Where Chap. 2 established that pluralistic knowledge emerges through situated perspectives in dialogue, Chap. 3 demonstrates how this same architecture addresses the practical challenges of explainability (making AI decisions transparent and understandable) and contestability (enabling meaningful challenge and revision). FOAM's differentiated agents, each anchored in explicit stance vectors, transform the black-box problem by making the situatedness of AI reasoning visible rather than hidden. Moreover, its sublation operators ensure that explanations preserve rather than erase the productive tensions that generate robust understanding. Through rhetorical argumentation frameworks, this chapter reveals how Port Aquilo's climate council process provides a template for AI systems that are simultaneously explainable and contestable.

This chapter's central question is: How can plural, rhetorically aware multi-agent systems produce simultaneously explainable and contestable decisions?

The chapter examines dual accountability challenges, rhetorical argumentation frameworks, multi-agent implementations, and practical contestability mechanisms.

3.2 The Dual Challenges of Explainability and Contestability

3.2.1 *The Challenge of Authentic Explainability*

In 2016, ProPublica revealed that COMPAS, a widely used algorithm for predicting criminal recidivism, was producing risk scores that judges could neither understand nor challenge meaningfully (Angwin et al., 2016). The system classified defendants as high or low risk for reoffending. However, it provided no clear explanation of how it reached these conclusions, and more troublingly, no mechanism for defendants or their attorneys to contest the algorithm's assessment. Similar patterns emerge across high-stakes AI applications: a medical AI recommends treatment protocols that doctors cannot adequately explain to patients, hiring algorithms make decisions based on factors that remain opaque to both applicants and HR professionals, and financial AI systems deny loans with explanations that sound plausible but may not reflect the system's actual reasoning process.

These failures reveal a fundamental problem with current approaches to AI accountability. While the demand for "explainable AI" has grown dramatically, most existing solutions provide post- hoc rationalizations, plausible narratives constructed after decisions are made, that may bear little relationship to the system's actual decision-making process (Rudin, 2019). Even when explanations are provided, users typically lack effective mechanisms to challenge or revise AI decisions. This dual failure of explainability and contestability threatens democratic accountability as AI systems increasingly influence critical decisions in healthcare, criminal justice, education, and employment.

The core challenge is that current AI systems are designed around a paradigm of singular, authoritative decision-making. A single model produces a single answer, potentially accompanied by a single explanation. This approach fundamentally misaligns with how complex decisions are made in democratic societies, where multiple perspectives are brought into dialogue, assumptions are challenged, and decisions remain open to revision based on new evidence or changing values.

As AI models become increasingly sophisticated and opaque, there is a pressing demand for methods to understand their decision-making processes. Legal frameworks, such as the EU's GDPR, mandate transparency in automated decision-making (European Union, 2016).

Recent breakthroughs in AI interpretability research, such as Anthropic's "AI microscope" approach and DeepMind's Gemma Scope sparse autoencoders, have begun to reveal the inner workings of large language models (Anthropic, 2025; Lieberum et al., 2024). However, interpretability work rarely reaches end-users, most affected by algorithmic decisions. This gap is well-documented: Haque et al. (2023) found that only 58 out of 1707 papers on explainable AI explicitly addressed the end-user perspective.

Explainability is not monolithic. Yao (2021) highlights different types of explanations, categorized along Mechanistic-Social and Particular-General axes:

Yao's Taxonomy of Explanations

	Particular	*General*
Mechanistic	**Diagnostic**: Why did the system produce this specific output for this input?	**Expectation**: What general patterns and behaviors can I expect from this system?
Social	**Explication**: How can this output be made understandable to humans?	**Role**: How do we justify using this system in its social context?

This plurality in explanatory needs demonstrates that a single explanation approach cannot satisfy all stakeholders or contexts. As Yao notes, "adopting the view of explanatory pluralism means that we do not place primacy on any one type of explanation but acknowledge that there are many types, each suiting a different context or need." This insight is crucial for developing truly pluralistic methods of explainability.

The Problem of Post-Decision Rationalization

A critical challenge concerns the authenticity of explanations: do post-decision rationalizations constitute genuine explainability, or are they fabricated justifications disconnected from actual decision-making processes? (Adebayo et al., 2022). This question gains significance as AI systems become increasingly complex, with decision-making processes that may not follow human-interpretable reasoning patterns.

Even post-hoc rationalizations serve essential functions: they must maintain plausible connections to decisions, create a tethering effect, initiate pressure for justifiable choices, and discipline the effect, thereby initiating contestable dialogue with dialogical value (Lombrozo, 2011; Weller, 2019).

However, critics argue that post-hoc explanations mislead users by creating a false understanding of the underlying process. Rudin (2019) advocates for inherently interpretable models rather than post-hoc explanations of black-box systems. This concern extends to Chain of Thought reasoning, where models articulate thinking processes before generating outputs. Recent Anthropic research shows that even when models explicitly describe their reasoning approach, these explanations may not accurately reflect the actual computational processes (Anthropic, 2024). This disconnection between stated reasoning and internal mechanisms reinforces the critique that explanations constructed after—or during—model decisions often fail to align with actual decision-making processes, risking deception or oversimplification.

This tension between explanatory fidelity and utility highlights the need for approaches that acknowledge the limitations of post-hoc explanations while maximizing their value through plural perspectives and contestability mechanisms.

3.2.2 *Contestability and its Interdependence with Explainability*

While explainability focuses on making AI decisions understandable, contestability addresses the critical need for these decisions to be challengeable. Contestability in AI refers to the ability of AI decisions and actions to be challenged, debated, and potentially revised, ensuring that AI systems are subject to ongoing evaluation and improvement rather than viewed as infallible (Leofante et al., 2024).

Cohen and Suzor (2024) argue that "public contestability is a critical attribute of governance arrangements designed to align AI deployment with the public interest." They identify three underlying requirements for effective contestability:

1. **Capabilities to organize**—the ability of affected stakeholders to collectively identify, articulate, and pursue challenges to AI systems
2. **Separation of powers**—the distribution of authority and decision-making capacity across different stakeholders and institutions
3. **Access to alternative and independent information**—the availability of diverse sources of information to support meaningful contestation

Contestability is not merely an extension of explainability but a distinct property that requires specialized mechanisms and frameworks. At the same time, explainability addresses the "what" and "how" of AI decisions, contestability addresses the "why not" and provides pathways for critique, challenge, and revision.

Recent advances in language model reasoning have begun operationalizing this "why not" questioning through self-reflective mechanisms. Recent advances enable models to engage in self-reflection and iterative improvement before committing to answers (Goyal et al., 2024; Shinn et al., 2023; Madaan et al., 2023). These approaches represent early steps toward systems that can not only explain their reasoning but also question initial responses, identify potential flaws, and iteratively improve, capabilities essential for meaningful contestability.

The Interconnected Nature of these Challenges

Explainability and contestability, while distinct, are deeply interconnected. Effective contestation requires understanding that only explainability can provide, while truly meaningful explainability must acknowledge the possibility of contestation. This interconnection is particularly evident in pluralistic contexts where multiple values and perspectives may be at play.

Kasirzadeh (2023) distinguishes between "first-order value choices (implementing specific accounts of values)" and "second-order value choices (determining the legitimacy of these first- order value selections)." This framework suggests that genuine pluralistic alignment requires explicit engagement with both levels, explaining the values being implemented and making transparent the authority by which those values were chosen.

This dual-level approach requires treating AI decisions as provisional hypotheses open to ongoing challenge.

3.3 Philosophical Foundations for Pluralistic AI

Chapter 2 established three philosophical principles that directly inform explainability and contestability design:

- **Dewey's Experimentalism** → *Iterative feedback loops*: AI explanations should be ongoing social processes, not static outputs. Decisions become hypotheses tested through stakeholder engagement (Dewey, 1927).

- **Haraway's Situated Knowledge** → *Stance disclosure*: Every AI perspective is partial and positioned. Systems must make their situatedness explicit through stance vectors and value transparency (Haraway, 1988).
- **Hegel's Dialectical Method** → *Debate-then-synthesis*: Contradictions generate new understanding. Multi-agent debate produces richer explanations than single authoritative voices. (Hegel, 1977)

Result: AI systems designed for dialogue, contestation, and productive tension, where decisions are provisional hypotheses open to ongoing challenge and revision. For a more detailed philosophical analysis, see Chapter 2, §§ 2.1–2.3.

3.4 Rhetorical Argumentation as a Framework for AI Pluralism

3.4.1 Defining Rhetorical Argumentation in the Context of AI

Rhetorical argumentation refers to the art of persuasion that focuses on tailoring arguments to specific audiences and contexts. In explainable AI, it enhances the system's ability to generate explanations that are both logically sound and compelling, tailored to users' needs and backgrounds. This approach bridges the gap between formal logical reasoning and human-centric communication, providing a complementary framework to computational argumentation (Grasso, 2003).

AI systems can systematically analyze arguments by breaking them down into "claims, grounds (evidence), warrants (logical connections), backing (support for warrants), qualifiers (limitations), and rebuttals" (Bauschard, 2024). Unlike human debaters, AI systems can "simultaneously evaluate and construct multiple argument structures," potentially deploying specialized sub-agents for each argumentation component.

This rhetorical capability enables AI systems to construct and analyze arguments in a way that enhances explainability. Consider an AI medical system: rather than simply stating its conclusion, a rhetorically informed system would present supporting evidence while acknowledging limitations and underlying values.

However, this rhetorical power raises ethical concerns about manipulation and the representation of diverse perspectives. To address these concerns, AI systems must include safeguards against manipulative rhetoric, such as agent honesty constraints and argument provenance logs that document the origins and transformations of data, making the sources and methods used to construct arguments transparent and accountable (Lin et al., 2022; Menon, 2025).

3.4.2 Computational Vs. Rhetorical Argumentation: A Comparative Framework

While computational argumentation provides formal structures for reasoning, rhetorical argumentation complements this by emphasizing the importance of diverse perspectives and contextual understanding.

Dimension	*Computational argumentation*	*Rhetorical argumentation*
Primary focus	Formal logical structures and validity	Persuasion and audience adaptation
Key strengths	• Rigorous logical consistency • Automated evaluation • Clear argument representation	• Audience-centered communication • Contextual sensitivity • Persuasive effectiveness
Methods	• Assumption-based argumentation (ABA) • Formal inference rules • Attack/defense relationships	• Ethos, pathos, logos • Toulmin's argument schema • Value-based appeals
Typical output	Formal proof trees, logical structures	Natural language explanations tailored to specific audiences
Evaluation criteria	Logical soundness, consistency	Persuasiveness, comprehensibility, and audience acceptance
Limitations	May be inaccessible to non-experts	Risk of manipulation; may sacrifice logical rigor for persuasion
Role in AI pluralism	Ensures formal correctness of reasoning	Makes diverse perspectives accessible to human stakeholders

Integration Opportunity: Combining these approaches addresses the dual needs of formal correctness and human understanding, exemplifying how pluralistic AI holds opposed approaches in productive tension.

Computational argumentation employs formal methods, such as assumption-based argumentation, for modeling structured debates (Toni,

2014). For example, in a medical diagnosis context, ABA might represent competing diagnostic hypotheses based on different assumptions about the significance of specific symptoms.

Rhetorical argumentation, in contrast, focuses on the persuasive aspects of communication and the adaptation of arguments to different audiences and contexts. This distinction is developed in the work of Walton and Gordon (2014), who propose formal models of "persuasion dialogues" and computational persuasion systems that treat arguments as tools for influencing audiences, emphasizing how dialogue structure and user modeling shape the effectiveness of persuasion.

Bench-Capon and Atkinson (2009) contribute a value-based argumentation framework, where arguments are supported by promoting specific values and ranked according to value priorities. Their work emphasizes that persuasive communication involves not only facts and logic but also appeals to normative frameworks, offering a rich model for AI systems that must explain or justify decisions in ethically complex contexts.

This integration creates systems that ensure formal correctness while making diverse perspectives accessible to stakeholders.

3.5 Multi-Agent Language Systems (MALS) for Explainability

3.5.1 Architectural Approaches to Implementing Pluralistic AI for Explainability

Multi-Agent Language Systems (MALS) offer a concrete architecture for implementing AI pluralism, thereby enhancing explainability and accountability. These systems operationalize the three FOAM primitives introduced in Chap. 2: differentiated agents (distinct perspectives with explicit stance vectors), deliberative protocols (structured critique exchanges), and sublation operators (synthesis that preserves rather than erases tension).

Plurals as FOAM Implementation

Ashkinaze et al.'s Plurals system illustrates a direct instantiation of FOAM's architecture. Plurals implements differentiated agents through large language models (LLMs) with distinct personas, drawing on government datasets to create nationally representative viewpoints. Its deliberative protocols manifest as customizable "Structures"—debate patterns, brainstorms, and voting procedures inspired by deliberative democracy theory. The system's Moderators function as rudimentary sublation operators, summarizing discussions and guiding synthesis while maintaining plurality rather than forcing consensus (Ashkinaze et al., 2024).

Debate Systems as Partial FOAM
Irving et al.'s "AI safety via debate"represents a more straightforward FOAM implementation focused primarily on deliberative protocols. The system instantiates differentiated agents through two AI opponents taking contrary positions, engages them through structured adversarial dialogue (deliberative protocols), but implements only basic sublation, as human judges select winners rather than preserving productive tensions (Irving et al., 2018). This approach demonstrates FOAM's potential while highlighting the importance of more sophisticated sublation mechanisms that maintain rather than eliminate dissent.

Dylan's Dynamic Architecture
Liu et al.'s Dynamic LLM-Agent Network (DyLAN) offers an alternative approach to FOAM's sublation operators. Where FOAM preserves tension through composite proposals with dissent memos, DyLAN creates emergent synthesis through dynamic reconfiguration—differentiated agents with specialized roles engage through flexible deliberative protocols that adapt based on task requirements. The system's ability to restructure itself represents a more fluid approach to sublation, where synthesis emerges from evolving agent interactions rather than formal mediation processes (Liu et al., 2024).

These architectural approaches demonstrate that FOAM's primitives can be implemented with varying degrees of sophistication and different balances between structure and flexibility, each offering distinct advantages for explainability and contestability goals.

3.5.2 Types of Diversity in Multi-Agent Systems

In multi-agent language systems, diversity manifests across multiple dimensions, each contributing to the system's overall cognitive capabilities and explanatory power. To illustrate how these dimensions work in practice, consider a diabetes management AI assistant designed to help patients and doctors make treatment decisions:

Agent A—Clinical Evidence Specialist

- *Architectural diversity*: Transformer-based model optimized for processing clinical literature
- *Training diversity*: Fine-tuned on medical research databases and clinical trials
- *Functional diversity*: Specializes in evidence-based medicine and statistical analysis
- *Perspective diversity*: Prioritizes empirical evidence and clinical efficacy

Agent B—Patient Advocate

- *Architectural diversity*: Conversational AI model with enhanced emotional intelligence
- *Training diversity*: Trained on patient narratives and quality-of-life studies
- *Functional diversity*: Focuses on patient experience and lifestyle integration
- *Perspective diversity*: Emphasizes patient autonomy and treatment acceptability

Agent C—Resource Optimizer

- *Architectural diversity*: Mixture-of-experts model with specialized cost analysis sub- networks
- *Training diversity*: Exposed to health economics data and insurance policies
- *Functional diversity*: Analyzes cost-effectiveness and healthcare resource allocation
- *Perspective diversity*: Balances treatment effectiveness with economic feasibility

How Diversity Dimensions Manifest

1. **Architectural diversity** encompasses agents with distinct neural network structures, varying in terms of model ensemble (MoE) models, layer configurations, and specialized architectures.
2. **Training diversity** exposes agents to different datasets and training regimes, resulting in varied knowledge bases and processing styles.
3. **Functional diversity** assigns specialized roles through targeted fine-tuning on domain- specific datasets, explicit role-based prompting, or architectural modifications for particular cognitive tasks.

4. **Perspective diversity** implements systematic variation in training objectives, exposure to different cultural datasets, or application of different reasoning frameworks during inference.

System-Level Benefits
When a patient asks, "Should I switch from insulin injections to an insulin pump?" this diverse team provides a multifaceted response:

- **Agent A** presents clinical evidence on pump effectiveness in HbA1c reduction
- **Agent B** discusses lifestyle benefits and patient satisfaction data
- **Agent C** analyzes insurance coverage and long-term cost implications

Rather than a single authoritative recommendation, the system generates a rich dialogue that helps patients and doctors understand trade-offs and make informed decisions aligned with individual values and circumstances.

FOAM Primitive Mapping
These diversity dimensions directly support FOAM's architecture: architectural and training diversity create robust differentiated agents with genuinely distinct perspectives; functional diversity enables specialized deliberative protocols where agents can challenge each other's domain expertise; and perspective diversity provides the raw material for sublation operators to weave together competing viewpoints. The diabetes management example demonstrates how FOAM's three primitives work together—each agent's stance vector (clinical evidence, patient advocacy, resource optimization) creates the conditions for productive deliberation and emergent synthesis.

3.5.3 *Recent Research on Multi-Agent LLM Systems*

Recent research (2023–present) has turned to multi-agent large language model (LLM) frameworks as a path to more transparent and contestable AI reasoning. Instead of a single monolithic model producing an answer and a potentially post-hoc explanation, these approaches use multiple specialized or adversarial LLM agents whose interactions make the reasoning process explicit and self-correcting. By having agents either collaborate on different reasoning sub-tasks or debate each other's conclusions, the system's decision-making becomes visible as a dialogue or multi-step process, which users (or other agents) can scrutinize and intervene in.

One prominent line of work uses LLMs debating one another to refine answers. Du et al. (2023) demonstrate that a "*society of minds*" debate—where multiple LLM instances independently propose answers and then critique each other's reasoning over several rounds—significantly improves both reasoning accuracy and factual correctness, while reducing hallucinations (Du et al., 2023). By externalizing reasoning as arguments and counterarguments, this approach enables observers to trace how the final answer emerges from the discussion, thereby enhancing transparency. However, if all agents share similar training biases, such debates can converge on a wrong consensus. Addressing this, Liang et al. (2024) introduce a Multi-Agent Debate (MAD) strategy that encourages *dissent* and internal critique (Liang et al., 2024). In their framework, two LLM-based debaters engage in a tit-for-tat exchange, moderated by a judge agent, with the explicit aim of surfacing novel viewpoints. This setup combats the "degeneration-of-thought" effect (where a single model's self-reflection gets stuck on an incorrect assumption) by ensuring that others continually challenge each agent's claims. The result is more divergent, critical thinking within the system, and fewer reasoning errors (Liang et al., 2024).

Another approach to multi-agent explainability uses layered reasoning and verification. Sanwal (2025) proposes the *Layered Chain-of-Thought (CoT) prompting* framework, which breaks down a complex problem into a sequence of discrete reasoning layers, each checked by an independent process or agent before proceeding (Sanwal, 2025). For example, one agent may generate a partial solution for a sub-problem, and a different agent (or tool) immediately verifies that step against a knowledge source or rule base. By enforcing verification at every layer (rather than only reviewing the final answer), Layered-CoT catches contradictions or mistakes early and prevents faulty assumptions from propagating. This yields step-by-step explanations that are more *faithful* to the actual decision process. In essence, the chain-of-thought itself becomes a multi-agent, multi-stage conversation: specialized agents can serve as a "reasoner," a "checker," or even a "user proxy," injecting feedback at each step. The result is a transparent reasoning trail in which each intermediate inference is open to contestation (e.g., a verification agent can flag a flawed step and prompt a revision), dramatically improving the clarity and reliability of the final explanation (Sanwal, 2025).

Researchers are also combining role specialization and critique to enhance explainability. For instance, He et al. (2023) develop a multi-agent framework called *LEGO* for generating explanations of causality. In LEGO, one LLM agent, in the role of *Explainer*, produces an initial causal explanation, and another agent acts as *Critic*, rigorously analyzing and iteratively refining that explanation. This two-agent review process is akin to an internal peer review: the explainer's reasoning is made explicit and then *systematically contested* by the critic, leading to a final output that has survived rounds of scrutiny. Such an approach has been shown to yield more robust and trustworthy explanations, as any logical gaps or unsupported claims raised by the first agent are promptly identified and addressed by the second (Tran et al., 2025). As discussed in Sect. 3.5.1, Liu et al.'s (2024) Dynamic LLM-Agent Networks (DyLAN) exemplify how dynamic agent coordination can enhance explainability. Beyond its architectural innovations in sublation operators, DyLAN's approach to decomposing problem-solving across specialized agents makes the decision process inherently interpretable. Users can observe which sub- problem each agent solved and how their outputs influenced the final decision. The system's dynamic coordination ensures that "reasoning emerges from visible interactions" among the agents, with each interaction serving as an explainable step tailored to the context. This visibility into agent contributions clarifies why a particular answer was chosen and which knowledge sources informed different aspects of the rationale, demonstrating how multi-agent architectures can transform opaque reasoning into transparent, contestable processes.

Crucially, many of these multi-agent paradigms not only produce richer explanations but also actively enable contestability—the ability to challenge and revise the model's reasoning. Recent work by Freedman et al. (2024) exemplifies this trend by integrating formal argumentation techniques into LLM reasoning. In their *Argumentative LLM* framework, the model generates a structured graph of arguments and counterarguments for a decision, and a formally defined inference procedure then determines the outcome. Because the final answer is *grounded in an explicit argument graph*, there is a direct correspondence between the reasoning and the decision (addressing the common concern that LLM "explanations" may be decoupled from how the answer was produced). More importantly, this structure makes the system inherently contestable: if a human or another agent intervenes by adding a new argument, removing an incorrect premise, or adjusting the weight of an existing argument, the system will update the outcome accordingly (Freedman et al., 2024). In other words, the decision is not a fixed output of an opaque model, but a *negotiable hypothesis* subject to evidence and reasoning that anyone (or any agent) can critique. This guarantee of contestability, also evident in debate-centric systems, transforms the AI from an oracle into a collegial reasoner whose conclusions can be audited and challenged in real-time.

In summary, the latest multi-agent LLM systems contribute to explainable and contestable AI by making reasoning a multi-person (or multi-agent) process. Techniques such as agent debates, layered verification of chain-of-thought, and role-based argumentation compel the model to *demonstrate its reasoning* and consider alternative viewpoints before finalizing an answer. This not only yields more transparent rationales but also embeds a mechanism for internal critique and error correction—if one agent strays or reasons poorly, another can call it out. The upshot is an AI that is not only able to explain its decisions but also one whose decisions are *arrived at through explanation* and open deliberation. These developments mark a significant step toward AI systems that are both understandable in their operation and contestable in their outcomes, aligning with the broader goals of trustworthy and accountable AI (Sanwal, 2025).

3.6 Debate-Centered Approaches to Contestability

Returning to the Port Aquilo council in Chap. 2, imagine if residents could query the mediation graph in real-time—challenging Marè's oceanographic projections with local flood observations, or contesting Aequitas's financing assumptions with alternative economic models. This interactive contestability transforms AI deliberation from a closed process into an ongoing public dialogue where affected stakeholders can meaningfully challenge and reshape the reasoning that governs their lives.

3.6.1 *Debate as a Mechanism for Implementing Contestability*

AI pluralism offers a robust model for contestability by fostering diverse viewpoints and promoting debate among AI agents. The differentiation of AI agents based on individual perspectives inherently supports contestability, allowing multiple, potentially conflicting views to coexist. By designing AI systems capable of questioning their assumptions and engaging in genuine dialogue, we create a framework where AI decisions are not just explainable but also open to challenge and revision.

Debate serves as a crucial mechanism for realizing the potential of AI pluralism and ensuring the contestability of AI decisions and explanations. When diverse agents engage in dialectical exchanges, they can challenge each other's decisions and reasoning, leading to a more thorough examination of the issues.

Irving et al.'s "AI safety via debate"provides a concrete example of how debate can be implemented as a contestability mechanism (Irving et al., 2018). In this framework, two AI agents engage in an adversarial dialogue about a question or task, with a human judge overseeing the debate and determining which agent's argument is more convincing. The intended outcome is that through the debate, any misleading or incorrect reasoning by one agent will be called out by the other, allowing the judge to discern the truth more easily. Initial empirical results were promising: in an MNIST image classification experiment where agents competed to convince a sparse classifier, debate boosted the classifier's accuracy from 59.4% to 88.9% given 6 pixels, and from 48.2% to 85.2% given 4 pixels (Irving et al., 2018).

This approach treats AI decisions as testable hypotheses subject to collective scrutiny. For safety-specific performance data on debate protocols, see Chap. 5.

3.6.2 *Key Structures for AI Debate Systems*

Several key structures can be implemented to facilitate effective debate in AI systems, each offering different advantages and addressing different aspects of contestability:

Structured debates among AI agents involve creating protocols that govern how different AI agents can engage in formal debates, including debate length limits, structured turn-taking with defined roles (proposer, critic, and mediator), evidence presentation standards and citation requirements, and rebuttal mechanisms and criteria for successful challenges.

Human-in-the-loop debate frameworks involve humans as judges or participants in the debate process, with clear instructions for judges that specify evaluation criteria, mechanisms for requesting clarification or additional information, tie-breaking criteria for cases where arguments are equally compelling, and methods for differentiating between factual disputes and value disagreements.

Hybrid approaches that combine expert input and agent interaction integrate external expertise into the debate process, incorporating processes for soliciting expert input at critical junctures, methods for incorporating diverse disciplinary perspectives, and mechanisms for identifying when additional expertise is needed.

Ashkinaze et al.'s Plurals system demonstrates a structured approach to AI deliberation that can be adapted for debate-centered contestability. The system organizes interactions through Structures (patterns of interaction, such as debates, brainstorms, or votes) and Moderators (components that summarize or guide the discussion) (Ashkinaze et al., 2024). By grounding these in deliberative democracy literature, the system aims for AI outputs that reflect a plurality of viewpoints rather than a homogenized answer.

The effectiveness of these structures depends on their ability to create genuine spaces for contestation, where challenges are not merely registered but meaningfully addressed and engaged with. This requires attention to power dynamics, ensuring that all perspectives can be heard and considered, as well as transparency about the debate process, including clarification of the rules, roles, and criteria used to structure and evaluate the debate.

3.6.3 Rhetorical Strategies in AI Debate

Rhetorical strategies can be employed to enhance the effectiveness of argumentation and ensure that diverse perspectives are represented and considered:

Claim-evidence-warrant-backing structures: Following Toulmin's model of argumentation (Toulmin, 1958/2003), AI agents can structure their arguments with explicit claims, supported by evidence, connected by warrants (logical connections), and strengthened by backing (support for warrants).

Value hierarchies in argumentation: AI agents can explicitly acknowledge the values underlying their arguments and how they are prioritized, making the normative assumptions of their reasoning transparent and open to challenge.

Managing ethical pluralism in contestation: As highlighted by Rudschies et al. (2021), different stakeholders may prioritize different ethical principles. Debate systems can incorporate mechanisms to ensure diverse ethical perspectives are represented and considered in the contestation process.

These rhetorical strategies create the conditions for a productive dialectical process that does not merely seek to defeat opposing viewpoints but to engage with them in a way that leads to a higher synthesis or sublation.

An illustrative dialogue showing rhetorical moves in an AI debate might include:

Agent A (Medical decision support): "Based on the patient's presenting symptoms and medical history, I recommend Treatment X because it has shown a 78% efficacy rate in clinical trials for similar cases." [Claim with evidence].

Agent B (Patient advocate): "While efficacy is important, Treatment X requires a lengthy hospital stay, which would be difficult for this patient given their family responsibilities. We should consider Treatment Y, which has 65% efficacy but can be administered outpatient—the tradeoff of slightly lower efficacy for significantly improved quality of life seems justified for this patient's profile." [Value-based challenge with alternative].

This dialogue demonstrates how rhetorical strategies can be employed to make contestation more productive, with agents explicitly acknowledging the evidential basis for their claims, the values informing their recommendations, and the potential tradeoffs involved. For a complete worked example of how pluralist debate can be internalised as a safety architecture—with sentinel, fairness, and whistle-blower roles—see Chap. 5.

3.7 Implementing Contestability Mechanisms in Practice

3.7.1 Technical Frameworks for Contestable AI

To effectively implement contestability in AI systems through pluralistic approaches, several practical mechanisms can be employed:

1. **Argumentation Frameworks**: Implementing structured frameworks, such as Toulmin's model or assumption-based argumentation (ABA), within AI systems enables formalized debates and reasoned exchanges of viewpoints.
2. **Transparent Decision Logs**: Maintaining comprehensive logs of AI decision-making processes that stakeholders can access and review, including alternative options and reasoning paths.

3. **Interactive User Interfaces**: Developing interfaces that enable stakeholders to probe AI reasoning, pose challenges, and request clarification or additional information.
4. **Feedback Mechanisms**: Implementing structured channels for stakeholders to provide feedback on AI decisions and explanations, creating an ongoing dialogue rather than a one-time explanation.

These technical frameworks should address Cohen and Suzor's three requirements for effective contestability: organizing capabilities, separation of powers, and access to alternative and independent information (Cohen & Suzor, 2024). These frameworks can support meaningful contestability by providing mechanisms for stakeholders to coordinate contestation efforts, ensuring appropriate distribution of decision-making power, and providing access to necessary information.

3.7.2 Design Principles for Contestable Systems

Developing contestable AI systems requires adherence to key design principles that ensure these systems are accessible, adaptable, and accountable to diverse stakeholders:

Accessibility to diverse stakeholders: Mechanisms should enable meaningful engagement across expertise levels.

Adaptability to different expertise levels: The system should provide various levels of detail and explanation based on the user's expertise and information needs, potentially offering technical explanations for specialists and more accessible explanations for general users.

Tracking of contestation processes: Records of contestation processes should be maintained, including arguments presented, evidence considered, and outcomes, thereby creating an audit trail that informs future improvements and ensures accountability.

Accommodating value pluralism: The system should recognize and accommodate diverse values and perspectives, explicitly acknowledging normative assumptions and creating space for value-based challenges. Established frameworks such as Value-Sensitive Design (Friedman & Nissenbaum, 1996) and Community-in-the-Loop methodologies (Häußermann & Lütge, 2022) offer practical strategies for integrating diverse, potentially conflicting stakeholder values into technical design processes.

This emphasis on embedding contestability into system design is echoed by Alfrink et al. (2023), who offer a comprehensive framework for "Contestable AI by Design." Their work demonstrates that contestability is not a single feature, but a quality distributed across interfaces, workflows, and governance mechanisms. Kudina and van de Poel (2024) further reinforce the need to treat contestability as a sociotechnical property, arguing that AI systems must align with individual users and broader institutional structures, including policy environments and cultural norms.

3.7.3 Case Studies of Implemented Contestability Mechanisms

While full implementations of contestable AI systems are still emerging, several case studies provide insights into how contestability mechanisms can be implemented in practice:

FairPlay: This tool supports "collaborative auditing of algorithms for ethical concerns, particularly fairness" (Behzad et al., 2024). FairPlay highlights the challenge of meeting all fairness criteria simultaneously and the need for context-specific audits by diverse teams. Its interactive visualizations make complex algorithmic decisions more accessible and contestable, allowing users to explore how different variables influence outcomes and how various fairness metrics may conflict with one another.

Anthropic's Constitutional AI: This approach utilizes explicit normative principles to guide AI responses, thereby fostering internal debate and critique mechanisms within AI models (Bai et al., 2022). By incorporating multiple viewpoints and hypothetical conversations before generating a response, Constitutional AI enables a form of internal contestation within the AI system. It uses a set of principles or "constitution" to guide the system's outputs, creating a form of self-regulation where the system critiques its initial responses based on these principles.

Columbia Convening on AI Openness and Safety: This 2024 convening developed a research agenda grounded in openness and community-centered pluralism (Bdeir et al., 2024). Their work highlighted the need for decentralized, culturally and linguistically diverse safety tools with robust auditability mechanisms, offering a concrete institutional model for embedding pluralistic contestability into AI safety frameworks.

The following comparative table highlights the strengths and weaknesses of these approaches:

Approach	*Strengths*	*Weaknesses*	*Key contestability features*
FairPlay	Interactive visualizations; collaborative auditing; multiple fairness metrics	Limited to fairness concerns; requires technical knowledge	Visual comparison of outcomes; team-based review process; multiple metrics for evaluation
Constitutional AI	Internal self-critique; principle-based evaluation; scalable to many domains	Limited to pre-defined principles; primarily internal contestation	Principle-based review; hypothetical critiques; revision of initial outputs
Columbia convening	Community-centered approach; cultural/linguistic diversity; institutional framework	Early-stage conceptual model; limited implementation details	Decentralized oversight, diverse stakeholder inclusion, auditability mechanisms

These case studies demonstrate that implementing contestability mechanisms in practice requires a combination of technical tools, collaborative processes, and institutional support. They show the feasibility of developing AI systems that are open to challenge and revision, contributing to more transparent, accountable, and ethically sound AI. However, large-scale deployment will require governance structures that allocate responsibility for maintaining contestability over time.

3.8 Integration with Computational Argumentation

3.8.1 Complementary Strengths of Computational and Rhetorical Approaches

Integrating computational argumentation with rhetorical approaches can lead to more robust and inclusive AI systems that combine formal rigor with human-centric communication.

Computational argumentation offers several strengths:

- **Formal rigor and logical soundness**: Computational approaches provide well-defined frameworks for constructing and evaluating arguments, ensuring that reasoning is logically coherent and free from formal fallacies.

- **Clear representation of argument structures**: These approaches offer explicit representations of arguments and their relationships, making the reasoning process more transparent and easier to analyze.
- **Automated evaluation of argument acceptability**: Computational frameworks enable the automated assessment of which arguments are acceptable given a set of assumptions and attack relationships.

Rhetorical argumentation, meanwhile, contributes:

- **Audience-centered explanations** tailored to stakeholders with varying expertise, interests, and values.
- **Contextual sensitivity** to different situations and needs, recognizing that the relevance and persuasiveness of arguments depend on the specific context.
- **Persuasive framing** that enhances understanding and acceptance, making arguments not only logically sound but also compelling and accessible to human users.

As established in Sect. 3.4.2, computational and rhetorical argumentation offer complementary strengths: formal rigor versus audience adaptation, automated evaluation versus persuasive communication. Integrating these approaches creates AI systems that are both logically sound and effectively communicated.

3.8.2 Integration Strategies

Integrating computational and rhetorical approaches to argumentation can be achieved through several strategies that preserve the strengths of each while addressing their respective limitations:

1. **Hybrid frameworks combining formal logic and rhetorical elements**: These frameworks maintain the formal rigor of computational argumentation while incorporating rhetorical elements to enhance accessibility and persuasiveness.
2. **Translating between computational and human-interpretable arguments**: Systems can translate between formal representations used in computational argumentation and more natural, rhetorically informed explanations accessible to human users.

3. **Multi-level explanation systems**: These systems provide explanations at multiple levels of abstraction, from detailed formal representations for technical users to higher-level summaries for non-experts.
4. **Context-sensitive argumentation**: Integrated systems can adapt their argumentation strategies based on the specific context and audience, employing different rhetorical techniques for different users or situations.
5. **Toulmin schema auto-generation**: LLM agents can be trained to automatically generate arguments based on Toulmin's model, including explicit claims, evidence, warrants, backing, qualifiers, and rebuttals. This process must account for potential failure modes, such as missing or inadequate warrants connecting evidence to claims, overgeneralization from limited evidence, and conflation of factual and normative claims.

As Vassiliades, Bassiliades, and Patkos note, argumentation can be integrated with explainable AI to enhance the trustworthiness and understandability of AI systems (Vassiliades et al., 2021). They suggest that argumentation can provide a framework for organizing and presenting explanations in a way that is more accessible and persuasive to human users, bridging the gap between formal reasoning and human-centric communication.

Existing hybrid models demonstrate integration strategies through mixed-initiative decision support and structured debate systems (Van den Bosch & Bronkhorst, 2018; McBurney & Parsons, 2009).

Rahwan's "Society-in-the-Loop" framework (2018) articulates a normative vision for AI governance in which algorithmic decisions are not only explainable but publicly contestable through institutional feedback loops. This aligns with the pluralistic argumentation model advocated in this chapter, where AI outputs are provisional and open to continuous challenge by multiple stakeholders.

3.8.3 Connecting Integration to Contestability Goals

The integration of computational and rhetorical approaches directly supports the contestability objectives outlined throughout this chapter. By combining formal logical rigor with persuasive, accessible communication, integrated systems enable more effective challenge and revision processes.

Formal computational frameworks ensure that contestation is grounded in logical principles, while rhetorical elements make the contestation process accessible to diverse stakeholders with varying levels of technical expertise. This dual approach addresses the fundamental challenge of creating AI systems that are both technically sound and democratically accountable.

The success of integrated approaches ultimately depends on their ability to facilitate meaningful dialogue between AI systems and human stakeholders, enabling genuine contestation that can lead to improved decisions and greater public trust in AI systems.

3.9 Conclusion and Research Agenda

AI pluralism provides a crucial link between technical interpretability and democratic accountability, creating genuinely explainable and meaningfully contestable AI systems. The integration of AI pluralism with rhetorical argumentation and computational frameworks enhances both explainability and contestability, leading to more robust and ethically sound AI systems. Rhetorical argumentation offers tools for crafting persuasive, contextually appropriate explanations. At the same time, debate offers a framework for exchanging and evaluating these explanations among multiple AI agents or between AI and human users. Pluralistic architectures make epistemic humility a design feature rather than an afterthought.

Rather than treating AI decisions as final verdicts, this approach treats them as provisional hypotheses open to ongoing challenge through pluralistic deliberation. This shift addresses the fundamental accountability failures that plague current AI systems.

3.10 Evaluation Metrics for Pluralistic AI Systems

To move beyond conceptual claims, concrete evaluation metrics are needed:

Quantitative metrics:

- Explanation of satisfaction surveys that measure user understanding and trust

- Contestation success rate: percentage of challenges that lead to revised outputs
- Correction frequency: how often the system updates its reasoning or conclusions
- Time-to-resolution: how quickly contestation processes reach satisfactory conclusions
- Diversity index: quantifying the range of perspectives represented in explanations

Qualitative metrics:

- Argument diversity assessment: evaluating the range of viewpoints and reasoning approaches
- Dialectical coherence: assessing how well different perspectives are integrated
- Value representation: examining whether diverse ethical frameworks are represented
- Accessibility evaluation: assessing how understandable explanations are to different stakeholders
- Contestation quality: evaluating the substantive engagement with challenges

3.10.1 Concrete Research Agenda

Future research in this area should focus on three testable hypotheses:

1. **Hypothesis 1**: Multi-agent systems with explicit rhetorical frameworks produce explanations that non-expert users find more satisfying and actionable than single-agent or non-rhetorical systems.

    - **Proposed benchmark**: A standardized explanation evaluation task across multiple domains (e.g., healthcare, finance, legal) with diverse user populations

2. **Hypothesis 2**: Debate-centered contestability mechanisms lead to more frequent and substantive revisions of AI decisions than passive feedback mechanisms.

- **Proposed benchmark**: A controlled comparison of different contestation approaches on a standardized set of challenging decision scenarios

3. **Hypothesis 3**: Integrating computational and rhetorical argumentation enhances the logical soundness and persuasiveness of AI explanations compared to either approach alone.

    - **Proposed benchmark**: An argumentation quality assessment framework that evaluates both formal correctness and rhetorical effectiveness

Implementing this research agenda will require:

- Creating open datasets of plural explanations for benchmark tasks
- Developing evaluation protocols that account for diverse stakeholder perspectives
- Building open-source toolkits for implementing and evaluating pluralistic AI systems
- Organizing workshops and challenges to foster collaboration and advance the field

3.10.2 Policy and Implementation Context

This research agenda aligns with ongoing efforts by public and private institutions to operationalize AI governance. The European Union's AI Act (2021) includes explicit requirements for human oversight, transparency, and the right to contest automated decisions— principles directly tied to the pluralist and contestability frameworks advanced in this chapter. Similarly, IBM's AI Ethics Guidelines (2021) emphasize principles of explainability, fairness, robustness, and accountability, offering a corporate roadmap for the ethical deployment of AI.

These legislative and corporate developments reflect a growing consensus that AI systems must be interpretable and institutionally accountable. The frameworks underscore the practical importance of the proposed research agenda and reinforce this chapter's claim that AI pluralism and rhetorical contestability are not only theoretical ideals but essential pillars for the responsible design of future AI systems.

By advancing this agenda, we can move beyond theoretical discussions of AI pluralism to create concrete implementations that enhance both the explainability and contestability of AI systems, fostering more transparent, accountable, and ethically aligned artificial intelligence that can meaningfully engage with the plurality of values in democratic societies.

References

Adebayo, J., Muelly, M., Liccardi, I., & Been Kim. (2022, December 9). Post hoc explanations may be ineffective for detecting unknown spurious correlations. *arXiv*. https://doi.org/10.48550/arXiv.2212.04629

Alfrink, K., Keller, I., Kortuem, G., & Doorn, N. (2023). Contestable AI by design: Towards a framework. *Minds and Machines, 33*(4), 613–639. https://doi.org/10.1007/s11023-022-09611-z

Angwin, J., Larson, J., Mattu, S., & Kirchner, L. (2016). Machine Bias: There's software used across the country to predict future criminals. And it's biased against blacks. ProPublica, May 23, 2016.

Anthropic. (2025, March 27). Tracing the thoughts of a large language model.. https://www.anthropic.com/research/tracing-thoughts-language-model.

Anthropic. (2024). *Reasoning models do not express their thoughts*. Anthropic Research. https://www.anthropic.com/research/reasoning-models-dont-say-think

Ashkinaze, M., Chaudhary, S., & Morris, M. R. (2024). Plurals: A system for pluralistic AI deliberation. In *Proceedings of the 2024 CHI Conference on Human Factors in Computing Systems* (pp. 1–15).

Bai, Y., Kadavath, S., Kundu, S., Askell, A., Kernion, J., Jones, A., Chen, A., Goldie, A., Mirhoseini, A., McKinnon, C., Amodei, D., Kaplan, J., Clark, J., Tran-Johnson, E., Irving, G., Amodei, D., Joseph, N., Hatfield-Dodds, S., Mann, B., … Brown, T. (2022). Constitutional AI: Harmlessness from AI feedback. *arXiv*. https://arxiv.org/abs/2212.08073

Bauschard, S. (2024). *AIs as rhetorical agents: Emerging superhuman communicators*. Substack. https://stefanbauschard.substack.com/p/ais-as-rhetorical-agents-emerging

Bdeir, A., François, C., & Pèran, L. (2024, December 19). A different take on AI safety: A research agenda from the Columbia convening on AI openness and safety. *Mozilla Blog*. https://blog.mozilla.org/en/mozilla/ai/columbia-convening-research-agenda/

Behzad, T., Singh, M. K., Ripa, A. J., & Mueller, K. (2024, December). FairPlay: A collaborative approach to mitigate bias in datasets for improved AI fairness. In *Proceedings of the 38th Conference on Neural Information Processing Systems (NeurIPS, 2024)*.

Bench-Capon, T. J. M., & Atkinson, K. (2009). Abstract argumentation and values. In *Argumentation in artificial intelligence* (pp. 45–64). Springer. https://doi.org/10.1007/978-0-387-98197-0_3
Cohen, J., & Suzor, N. (2024). Contesting the public interest in AI governance. *AI & SOCIETY, 39*(1), 307–321.
Dewey, J. (1927). *The public and its problems.* Henry Holt and Company.
Du, Y., Li, S., Torralba, A., Tenenbaum, J. B., & Mordatch, I. (2023). Improving factuality and reasoning in language models through multi-agent debate. *arXiv.* https://arxiv.org/abs/2305.14325
European Union. (2016). Regulation (EU) 2016/679 of the European Parliament and of the council of 27 April 2016 (general data protection regulation). *Art, 14.* https://eur-, lex.europa.eu/legal-content/EN/TXT/?uri=CELEX%3A32016R0679.
European Commission. (2021). *Proposal for a regulation of the European Parliament and of the Council laying down harmonised rules on artificial intelligence (Artificial Intelligence Act) and amending certain Union legislative acts* (COM/2021/206 final). EUR-Lex. https://eur- lex.europa.eu/legal-content/EN/TXT/?uri=CELEX%3A52021PC0206
Freedman, G.., Dejl, A., & Gorur, D. (2024). *Argumentative large language models for explainable and contestable claim verification.* arXiv preprint arXiv:2405.02079. https://doi.org/10.48550/arXiv.2405.02079.
Friedman, B., & Nissenbaum, H. (1996). Bias in computer systems. *ACM Transactions on Information Systems, 14*(3), 330–347. https://doi.org/10.1145/230538.230561
Grasso, F. (2003). *Characterising rhetorical argumentation* [Doctoral dissertation, University of Liverpool].
Goyal, S., Ji, Z., Rawat, A. S., Menon, A. K., Kumar, S., & Nagarajan, V. (2024). Think before you speak: Training language models with pause tokens - *International Conference on Learning Representations (ICLR).*
Haque, A. B., Islam, A. N., & Mikalef, P. (2023). Explainable artificial intelligence (XAI) from a user perspective: A synthesis of prior literature and problematizing avenues for future research. *Technological Forecasting and Social Change, 186.*
Haraway, D. (1988). Situated knowledges: The science question in feminism and the privilege of partial perspective. *Feminist Studies, 14*(3), 575–599.
Häußermann, J. J., & Lütge, C. (2022). Community-in-the-loop: Towards pluralistic value alignment in AI development. *AI & Ethics, 2*(4), 579–592.
He, Z., Cao, P., Chen, Y., Liu, K., Li, R., Sun, M., & Zhao, J. (2023). LEGO: A multi-agent collaborative framework with role-playing and iterative feedback for causality explanation generation. In *Findings of the Association for Computational Linguistics: EMNLP 2023* (pp. 9142–9163). Association for Computational Linguistics.

Hegel, G. W. F. (1977). *Phenomenology of spirit* (A. V. Miller, Trans.). Oxford University Press. (Original work published 1807).

IBM. (2021). *IBM principles for trust and transparency*. https://www.ibm.com/policy/trust- transparency

Irving, G., Christiano, P., & Amodei, D. (2018). AI safety via debate. *arXiv*. https://arxiv.org/abs/1805.00899

Kasirzadeh, A. (2023). Plurality of value pluralism and AI value alignment. *Ethics and Information Technology, 25*(2), 1–15.

Kudina, O., & van de Poel, I. (2024). A sociotechnical system perspective on AI. *Minds and Machines, 34*(3), Article 21. https://doi.org/10.1007/s11023-024-09680-2

Leofante, F., Ayoobi, H., Dejl, A., Freedman, G., Gorur, D., Jiang, J., Paulino-Passos, G., Rago, A., Rapberger, A., Russo, F., Yin, X., Zhang, D., & Toni, F. (2024). Contestable AI needs computational argumentation. *AI Magazine, 44*(1), 109–128.

Liang, T., He, Z., Jiao, W., Wang, X., Wang,Y., Wang, R., Yang, Y., Shi, S., & Tu, Z. (2024). Encouraging divergent thinking in large language models through multi-agent debate. In *Proceedings of the 2024 Conference on Empirical Methods in Natural Language Processing* (pp. 17889–17904). Association for Computational Linguistics, November 12–16, 2024.

Lieberum, T., Rajamanoharan, S., Conmy, A., Smith, L., Sonnerat, N., Varma, V., Kramár, J., Dragan, A., Shah, R., & Nanda, N. (2024). *Open sparse autoencoders everywhere all at once on Gemma 2*. arXiv. https://arxiv.org/abs/2408.05147

Lin, S., Hilton, J., & Evans, O. (2022). TruthfulQA: Measuring how models mimic human falsehoods. In *Proceedings of the 60th Annual Meeting of the Association for Computational Linguistics* (pp. 3214–3252). https://doi.org/10.18653/v1/2022.acl-long.229

Liu, Z., Zhang, Y., Li, P., Liu, Y., & Yang, D. (2024). A dynamic LLM-agent network for task- oriented agent collaboration. *arXiv*. https://arxiv.org/abs/2310.02170

Lombrozo, T. (2011). The instrumental value of explanations. *Philosophy Compass, 6*(8), 539–551.

Madaan, A., Tandon, N., Gupta, P., Hallinan, S., Gao, L., Wiegreffe, S., et al. (2023). Self-refine: Iterative refinement with self-feedback. *Advances in Neural Information Processing Systems, 36*.

McBurney, P., & Parsons, S. (2009). Dialogue games for agent argumentation. In *Argumentation in Artificial Intelligence* (pp. 261–280). Springer.

Menon, S. R. (2025). Ethical AI starts with data provenance: A FATE perspective. *IJARASEM*. https://philarchive.org/archive/SHREAS-2

Rahwan, I. (2018). Society-in-the-loop: Programming the algorithmic social contract. *Ethics and Information Technology, 20*(1), 5–14. https://doi.org/10.1007/s10676-017-9430-8

Rudin, C. (2019). Stop explaining black box models for high-stakes decisions and use interpretable models instead. *Nature Machine Intelligence, 1*(5), 206–215. https://doi.org/10.1038/s42256-019-0048-x

Rudschies, C., Schneider, I., & Simon, J. (2021, March). Value pluralism in the AI ethics debate—Different actors, different priorities. *International Review of Information Ethics, 29*, 1–15.

Sanwal, M. (2025). *Layered chain-of-thought prompting for multi-agent LLM systems: A comprehensive approach to explainable large language models.* arXiv preprint arXiv:2501.18645v2. https://arxiv.org/abs/2501.18645

Shinn, N., Cassano, F., Berman, E., Gopinath, A., Narasimhan, K., & Yao, S. (2023). Reflexion: Language agents with verbal reinforcement learning. *Advances in Neural Information Processing Systems, 36.*

Toni, F. (2014). A tutorial on assumption-based argumentation. *Argument & Computation, 5*(1), 89–117.

Toulmin, S. E. (2003). *The uses of argument.* Cambridge University Press. (Original work published 1958).

Tran, K.-T., Dao, D., Nguyen, M.-D., Pham, Q.-V., O'Sullivan, B., & Nguyen, H. D. (2025). *Multi-agent collaboration mechanisms: A survey of LLMs.* arXiv preprint arXiv:2501.06322v1.

van den Bosch, K., & Bronkhorst, A. W. (2018). Human-AI cooperation to benefit military decision-making. In *Proceedings of the NATO IST-160 Specialist's meeting on Big Data and Artificial Intelligence for Military Decision Making* (Bordeaux, France, May 30–June 1, 2018). NATO Science and Technology Organization. https://resolver.tno.nl/uuid:49e7b3ec-602f-4edd- a748-cf88a317e49d.

Vassiliades, A., Bassiliades, N., & Patkos, T. (2021). Argumentation and explainable artificial intelligence: A survey. *Knowledge Engineering Review, 36*, 1–30.

Walton, D., & Gordon, T. F. (2014). The Carneades model of argument invention. *Argumentation, 28*(2), 149–183. https://doi.org/10.1075/pc.20.1.01wal

Weller, A. (2019). Transparency: Motivations and challenges. In *Explainable AI: Interpreting, explaining and visualizing deep learning* (pp. 23–40). Springer.

Yao, Y. (2021). Explanatory Pluralism in Explainable AI. In: Holzinger, A., Kieseberg, P., Tjoa, A.M., Weippl, E. (eds) Machine Learning and Knowledge Extraction. CD-MAKE 2021. *Lecture Notes in Computer Science (LNISA)*, vol 12844. Springer. https://doi.org/10.1007/978-3-030-84060-0_18

PART II

AI Pluralism and Social Implications

CHAPTER 4

Foundational Theory and Technical Grounding for AI Pluralism

Devin Gonier

Abstract This chapter establishes the technical justification for AI Pluralism by arguing that diversity and synergy are a fourth fundamental axis of AI intelligence—orthogonal to model size, training data, and compute—enabling systems of interacting agents to achieve collective intelligence that surpasses what any monolithic approach can deliver. We formalize diversity through metrics like disagreement rates and semantic distance, while quantifying synergy via Partial Information Decomposition and O-Information—measuring emergent value that arises only through agent interaction. The chapter introduces practical interventions from lightweight prompting strategies to sophisticated architectures including representation engineering, multi-agent debate protocols, and Group Relative Policy Optimization (GRPO). We distinguish productive synergy, characterized by honest dialectical exchange where agents faithfully represent others' positions and acknowledge uncertainty, from deceptive interaction involving strawman arguments and selective evidence. Through structured debate frameworks and drawing on empirical findings from multi-agent research, we show how pluralistic systems can significantly outperform both individual agents and simple ensembles by fostering

D. Gonier (✉)
DebaterHub, Denver, CO, USA

P. A. Rao (ed.), *AI Pluralism*,
https://doi.org/10.1007/978-3-032-06558-2_4

genuine collaborative reasoning. The assessment framework provides concrete metrics for evaluating diversity-synergy tradeoffs, while future directions highlight evolution toward autonomous agents with persistent beliefs and shared memory systems. This technical blueprint enables practitioners to build AI systems that leverage collective intelligence through measured diversity and structured synergistic interaction.

Keywords AI Pluralism • Multi-agent systems • Diversity and synergy • Collective intelligence • Information decomposition • Multi-agent debate • Group Relative Policy Optimization (GRPO) • Representation engineering • Dialectical Reasoning • Partial Information Decomposition • O- Information • Emergent intelligence

4.1 Introduction: Bridging Theory and Implementation

Chapters 2 and 3 laid the conceptual groundwork for AI Pluralism. Chapter 1 presented pluralism as an epistemic ecology—an architectural alternative to monolithic AI, rooted in the philosophies of Dewey, Haraway, and Hegel, and visualized through Sloterdijk's foam metaphor. It highlighted the limitations of single-minded systems when facing complex, "messy" problems like the one in the Port Aquilo scenario.

The technical approaches here build directly on the explainability and contestability principles from Chap. 3, as well as the foundational concepts from Chap. 2. Achieving truly transparent and contestable AI Pluralism demands interpretable mechanisms for managing agent differentiation, coordination, and reasoning (Zhang et al., 2024). Inspired by Chap. 1's situated knowledge (Haraway) and experimental inquiry (Dewey), and Chap. 2's focus on rhetorical argumentation, the frameworks presented—from representation engineering to structured debate—foster the diversity needed for a robust epistemic ecology. They also provide clearer insights into how system outcomes emerge from distinct perspectives, enhancing transparency and enabling meaningful contestation.

4.2 Key Takeaways

This chapter provides the mathematical and computational foundations for AI Pluralism, formalizing diversity and synergy as a fourth axis of AI intelligence—orthogonal to model size, data, and compute.

Diversity reduces redundancy through uncorrelated errors and independent knowledge (like an orchestra with different instruments versus all violins), while synergy captures emergent information from agent interaction (like instruments playing complementary parts that harmonize versus playing the same melody). We quantify diversity via disagreement rates and semantic distance; synergy through Partial Information Decomposition and O-Information. This orthogonal axis enables continuous improvement through sophisticated agent interactions, unlike traditional scaling's diminishing returns.

Implementation ranges from lightweight prompting to deep architectural modifications including representation engineering and GRPO training. Productive synergy requires genuine dialectical exchange—faithful argument representation and epistemic humility, not mere interaction.

Assessment frameworks translate theory into practice: measuring diversity through output disagreement, synergy through performance gains exceeding simple ensembles. These metrics guide development of systems where collective intelligence emerges from structured interaction.

4.3 Theoretical Framework for AI Pluralism

The theoretical foundation of AI Pluralism rests on several key mathematical concepts that quantify the relationship between system diversity, computational resources, and intelligence. These concepts provide a rigorous framework for understanding how pluralistic systems can achieve superior performance compared to monolithic approaches, and why diversity and synergy should be treated as fundamental variables in AI design.

4.3.1 *Rethinking Intelligence: A Multi-Axis Framework*

Traditionally, intelligence in artificial systems has been modeled as a function of three primary variables:

1. **Model Size (S)**—usually measured by parameter count, governing representational capacity.

2. **Training Data Volume (D_T)**—the quantity and quality of data used during training, affecting generalization.
3. **Compute (C)**—encompassing both training and inference FLOPs, dictating how much raw processing is applied. Test time compute techniques like Tree of Thoughts, Chain of Thoughts, Self-Consistency etc.

This triad underpinned the "scaling laws" era (Kaplan et al., 2020), wherein model performance improved predictably with increases along all three axes. The Chinchilla paper (Hoffmann et al., 2022) refined this by showing that compute-optimal performance comes from balancing size and data, not maximizing one blindly.

However, even with these refinements, we are increasingly witnessing saturation in returns. Larger models (e.g., GPT-4, Gemini 1.5) now require exponentially more compute for linear performance improvements. Training budgets push the limits of energy consumption and accessibility, raising ecological, and equity concerns (Anthropic, 2024).

Crucially, unlike size, data, or compute—which operate on the scale of content ingestion or processing power—diversity and synergy operate on the **structuring of knowledge and reasoning**. They introduce qualitatively new dynamics, such as:

- multiple perspectives yielding different problem framings,
- adversarial collaboration revealing contradictions,
- recursive synthesis producing emergent concepts.

This fourth axis expands the design space of intelligence, raising the theoretical ceiling. Where monolithic scaling suffers diminishing returns, pluralistic systems continue to improve by exploring increasingly rich reasoning topologies and social-cognitive interactions among agents.

Consider a medical diagnosis scenario: A single AI doctor, no matter how large or well-trained, might miss crucial connections. But imagine a pluralistic system with an AI cardiologist, neurologist, endocrinologist, and general practitioner. Each brings distinct expertise (diversity), and their collaborative discussion often reveals insights none would reach alone (synergy). For instance, symptoms that individually suggest different conditions might, when discussed together, point to a rare metabolic disorder affecting multiple systems—a diagnosis emerging from their interaction, not from any single specialist's knowledge.

4.4 Formalizing Diversity (D) and Synergy (S)

The concepts of Diversity and Synergy have formal definitions rooted in information theory and ensemble learning, providing a rigorous basis for their role in AI Pluralism.

Diversity (D) generally refers to the independence or difference among multiple information sources or agents. In information-theoretic terms, diversity can be related to low mutual information or low correlation among agents' outputs. For a set of agents $A = A_1, \ldots, A_n$, diversity $D(A)$ can be quantified using various metrics. One approach relates to measures of similarity or correlation $\rho(A_i, A_j)$ between agents, where low similarity implies higher diversity.

Alternatively, Watanabe's total correlation measures the shared information among variables (Watanabe, 1960); a diverse set of agents would ideally have low total correlation, meaning each agent contributes information not fully redundant with the others. In the context of ensemble learning, diversity is often quantified by metrics like the pairwise disagreement rate (fraction of instances where two models differ) or the Q-statistic/correlation between model outputs.

Synergy (S) refers to information or capabilities that emerge from combining sources, beyond the sum of individual contributions. In Williams and Beer's Partial Information Decomposition (PID) framework (Williams & Beer, 2010), synergy is the information about a target Y that is only accessible jointly from multiple sources and not from any source alone. The PID framework decomposes the mutual information $I(Y; X_1, X_2, \ldots, X_n)$ into unique information from each source, redundant (overlapping) information shared by sources, and synergistic information.

Consider our medical AI team: when the rheumatologist notes rash patterns, the dermatologist observes joint swelling timing, and the internist highlights fever patterns, they collectively recognize lupus—a diagnosis unavailable to any single specialist. This is synergy: emergent insight from interaction.

Crucially, synergy requires honest exchange, not agreement:

Poor Synergy: Specialists undermine productive debate through strawman arguments ("So you think every joint pain is autoimmune?"), selective evidence citation, and rhetorical tricks to "win" rather than understand. This generates conflict without insight.

Good Synergy: The same specialists debate constructively. "The fever pattern seems inconsistent with lupus—how do you account for that?"

leads to specific evidence. "What if we're all wrong and this is drug-induced?" sparks medication review. They argue intensely but accurately represent positions, acknowledge uncertainty, and remain open to being wrong.

Through honest dialectical exchange, they reach deeper understanding.

The key: intellectual honesty—faithful representation of others' views, acknowledging contradictory evidence, and commitment to truth over winning. Technical frameworks must foster structured, honest dialectical exchange, not mere interaction.

In information theory terms, this is like the XOR problem: each individual bit (X_1 or X_2) has zero mutual information about the output (Y), yet the pair taken together X_1, X_2 has full information—the output is entirely synergistic ($I_{syn} > 0$, $I_{uniq1} = I_{uniq2} = I_{red} = 0$).

The O-Information (Ω) (Rosas et al., 2019) serves as a single quantitative index balancing redundancy and synergy. A positive Ω indicates redundancy dominates (variables largely overlap), while a negative Ω indicates net synergistic interactions. In synergy-dominated systems ($\Omega < 0$), each variable makes unique contributions that together yield more information than the sum of parts. In multi-agent AI, a negative O-information would suggest agents complement each other's knowledge or reasoning, producing insights only apparent from their collaboration.

4.5 Diversity and Synergy as Orthogonal Axes of Enhancement

The value of diversity is formally captured in ensemble learning theory. Krogh and Vedelsby (1995) (Krogh & Vedelsby, 1995) established the ambiguity decomposition for an ensemble of regression models:

$$E_{ens} = \bar{E} - \bar{D}$$

Where E_{ens} is the ensemble's mean-squared error, $\bar{E}$ is the mean error of the individual models, and $\bar{D}$ (the ambiguity) is the average variance of individual predictions around the ensemble mean. $\bar{D}$ quantifies the disagreement or diversity among the models' outputs. This equation shows that the ensemble error is lower than the mean individual error by an amount equal to this diversity term. This result formally established diversity as a second key factor (besides individual accuracy) in ensemble performance, demonstrating that improving collective accuracy requires diversity.

This creates a powerful implication: D and S are not substitutes for model size, but orthogonal contributors. **Orthogonality here means D and S contribute to model capability independently of the traditional scaling axes (parameters, compute, data). Just as Chain-of-Thought prompting unlocked reasoning improvements without additional training, D and S open qualitatively new pathways to intelligence.** As with Chain-of-Thought prompting, which added a qualitatively new dimension to LLM reasoning, increasing D and S opens up an entire new space of emergent capabilities (Wei et al., 2022). This includes collaborative inference, dialectical resolution, and distributed generalization.

In many cases, increasing D and S leads to performance improvements unachievable by scaling alone. Moreover, D and S interact multiplicatively: diversity provides independent hypotheses or approaches, and synergy emerges from their structured integration (e.g., debate, coordination, self-consistency).

4.6 Diversity and Synergy in Multi-Agent Intelligence

When multiple agents collaborate or compete, diversity and synergy substantially improve collective intelligence. In cooperative settings, a team of agents with complementary strengths or perspectives can solve problems that elude any single agent. Hong and Page (2004) (Hong & Page, 2004) proved that a group of diverse problem-solvers can outperform a like-sized group of the best-performing individuals under certain conditions, as diverse agents avoid the correlated failures that trap homogeneous experts.

Similarly, Marcolino et al. (2013) (Marcolino et al., 2013) showed that under proper aggregation rules, a diverse team of weaker agents can outperform a uniform team of stronger agents, demonstrating that the whole can be greater than the sum of its parts when those parts bring independent information or approaches. These results justify investing in diversity (D) as a means to increase the synergy (S) of the group.

In adversarial or mixed settings, diversity can similarly confer robustness and insight. The concept of “AI safety via debate“ exemplifies this, where agents critique each other's answers, making flaws more likely to be revealed. Recent research confirms that Multi-Agent Debate (MAD) strategies can improve truthfulness and reasoning in LLMs (Du et al., 2023). Each agent brings different potential misconceptions or partial knowledge, and their interactions generate more reliable conclusions than any one agent's first answer. Here, diversity in initial opinions combined with a synergistic dialectical process yields a more truthful outcome.

4.6.1 Techniques to Foster D and S

Several multi-agent interaction protocols and training techniques explicitly aim to increase diversity and harness synergy:

- **Debate and Dialectical Reasoning**: Forces agents to present alternative viewpoints and critique one another, injecting diverse perspectives and driving the joint system toward correct reasoning.
- **Chain-of-Thought Ensembles (Self-Consistency)**: Generating multiple independent reasoning chains from a single LLM and aggregating them leverages diversity in thought to cancel out idiosyncratic errors, analogous to model ensembles and finding correct answers more reliably.
- **Task Decomposition and Specialized Agents**: Splitting a complex task into subtasks handled by agents with different expertise (diversity in expertise) whose results are combined synergistically. This relates to Mixture-of-Experts ideas.
- **Epistemic Uncertainty Modeling**: Using ensembles of agents or models to estimate uncertainty via disagreement (as in disagreement-based active learning) helps identify knowledge gaps and guides exploration, ensuring the joint system acquires information synergistically.

4.7 A Unified Perspective and Mathematical Synthesis

The above frameworks can be conceptually unified by recognizing that pluralistic multi-agent systems aim to maximize the unique and synergistic information contributed by each component, while minimizing redundant overlap. Diversity (D) is valuable insofar as it reduces redundancy (uncorrelated errors, independent knowledge), and Synergy (S) is the positive gain attained when those diverse pieces interact to produce something novel or more accurate.

Using information decomposition, for two agents or models A_1 and A_2 working on a task with outcome Y, we can decompose the predictive information as:

$$I(Y;A_1,A_2) = I_{uniq1}(Y;A_1 \mid A_2) + I_{uniq2}(Y;A_2 \mid A_1) + I_{red}(Y;A_1;A_2) + I_{syn}(Y;A_1,A_2)$$

where I_{uniq1} and I_{uniq2} are the unique information contributions, I_{red} is the redundant (overlapping) information, and I_{syn} is the synergistic information. The goal of a pluralistic system is to maximize $I_{uniq1} + I_{uniq2} + I_{syn}$ while minimizing I_{red}. A truly pluralistic multi- agent system strives for an outcome where the whole has strictly more insight than any part ($I_{syn} > 0$).

This principle is evidenced by recent multi-LLM studies: for example, Hegazy (2024) showed that a diverse set of medium-sized LLMs debating a problem can outperform even a much larger single model, whereas using multiple copies of the same model did not yield as large a benefit. This gain is precisely the synergy at work. Likewise, the Mixture- of-Search-Agents (MoSA) framework found that multiple LLMs collaborating in a search process consistently outperformed a single LLM, demonstrating synergy in problem-solving by aggregating independent paths and refining them collaboratively.

In summary, the value of pluralistic multi-agent interaction can be formally justified through these lenses: diversity provides the raw material (uncorrelated, wide-ranging hypotheses or behaviors), and synergy quantifies the extra emergent value gained when these pieces are integrated. By designing systems to foster diversity and then actively combine ideas (through voting, debate, or coordination), we harness information or capabilities that no single agent—or simple bag of agents—would have.

The mathematical frameworks of ensemble diversity (Krogh & Vedelsby, 1995) and information decomposition (Williams & Beer, 2010) both support this conclusion: the optimal collective intelligence arises when we maximize the unique, non-redundant contributions of agents and leverage their synergy, rather than simply averaging their opinions. Such pluralistic systems can achieve higher reliability, creativity, and performance than even the strongest individual agent, proving that many minds can be better than one when diversity and synergy are properly quantified and utilized.

4.8 The Role of Metrics in System Design

Defining tractable, consistent metrics for D and S is essential for optimization. Metrics such as:

- Total correlation (for redundancy)
- Disagreement rate, entropy gap, or Q-statistic (for diversity)
- Partial Information Decomposition components (for synergy)
- O-Information as a system-level signal (Rosas et al., 2019)

enable measurable system improvement, agent specialization, and emergent task allocation. These metrics also tie into broader philosophical discussions of pluralism explored in later chapters, grounding epistemic pluralism in mathematically observable constructs.

4.9 Examples and Synthesized Equations

To illustrate the additive and multiplicative contributions of D and S, consider these examples:

- A CoT-enhanced single model (Ω_{base}): gains from depth of inference, but may still suffer from single-perspective failure.
- A team of redundant agents (low D, low S): behaves like an ensemble with limited improvement over the strongest member ($E_{ens} \approx \bar{E}$).
- A set of diverse agents (high D, low S): produces varied hypotheses but lacks integration—useful for exploration ($E_{ens} < \bar{E}$ due to diversity, but limited by lack of synergy).
- A dialectical system with both D and S: integrates diverse inputs via debate, leading to emergent conclusions not found in any single path ($I_{syn} > 0$).

This yields a generalized model for total intelligence (Ω_{total}):
$\Omega_{total} = \beta_0 \ln(S) + \beta_1 \ln(D_T) + \beta_2 \ln(C) + \alpha_1 D + \alpha_2 S + \alpha_3 DS$
Where:

- $\beta_0, \beta_1, \beta_2$ scale base factors

- α_1, α_2, α_3 capture dialectical gains

This framework sets the stage for the technical mechanisms that can realize D and S in practice. In the following section, we explore concrete technical approaches for implementing pluralistic AI systems, ranging from lightweight prompting strategies to deep architectural innovations.

4.10 Technical Interventions for AI Pluralism: Fostering Diversity

Cultivating meaningful diversity among agents or within a single system's reasoning processes is a prerequisite for building effective pluralistic AI systems. This requires deliberate technical interventions to create distinct perspectives, knowledge bases, reasoning styles, and capabilities. The approaches outlined here represent a spectrum of techniques for fostering such differentiation, ranging from lightweight methods applicable during inference to more integrated strategies involving model modification and data curation. These interventions lay the essential groundwork for the synergistic interactions discussed in the subsequent section.

4.10.1 Inducing Diversity Through Prompting and Inference-Time Techniques

Prompt engineering serves as the most direct and accessible method for inducing diverse perspectives in large language models without necessitating modifications to the underlying model weights. By carefully crafting system prompts or user instructions, a model can be guided to adopt a particular persona, role, or reasoning style, thereby simulating distinct viewpoints.

Simple techniques include explicit role specification, such as instructing the model to "Act as a skeptical scientist" or "You are an economist focused on market efficiency." More sophisticated approaches leverage few-shot examples to demonstrate the desired perspective.

For instance, in our medical diagnosis system, we might prompt different AI agents with: "You are a cautious diagnostician who always considers worst-case scenarios first."

Each prompt creates a different diagnostic approach. When a patient presents with chest pain, the cautious diagnostician immediately considers heart attack, the holistic practitioner asks about stress and diet, while the evidence-based physician requests specific cardiac enzyme tests. This diversity of initial approaches, achieved through simple prompting, ensures no important angle is overlooked.

Other techniques employ multi-path Chain-of-Thought prompting, where a single model generates multiple reasoning trajectories, each potentially steered toward a different line of argument or set of assumptions, thereby creating a form of internal diversity (OpenAI, 2024). While prompt-based methods offer minimal resource requirements and ease of implementation, the resulting diversity can sometimes be superficial, inconsistent, or constrained by the base model's inherent biases and training data, potentially failing to represent truly distinct underlying knowledge or reasoning structures.

Building upon prompting, **inference-time scaffolding** and the use of **structured thought templates** offer more refined ways to diversify reasoning paths without altering model parameters. Thought templates, essentially structured prompts or cues, are designed to nudge a model (or even a human) to consider additional angles or lines of reasoning. These templates can take various forms, including explicitly inviting counterarguments (e.g., using phrases like "Some might object that…" or "On the other hand…"), prompting hypothetical flips ("What if the opposite were true?"), or providing pros/cons scaffolds to encourage the listing of supporting and opposing points. Empirical evidence suggests that guided Chain-of-Thought exemplars incorporating questions and objections assist models in decomposing problems into sub-steps and considering edge cases, improving reasoning by prompting the articulation of implicit assumptions and the search for gaps, rather than premature convergence on a single conclusion.

Cognitive and rhetorical theories provide a strong theoretical basis for the effectiveness of these techniques. The argumentative theory of reason, proposed by Mercier and Sperber (Mercier & Sperber, 2011), suggests that human reasoning evolved not solely for discovering objective truth but for the generation and evaluation of arguments in social contexts. In debate-like settings, individuals are adept at considering multiple sides, while isolated reasoning is often susceptible to confirmation bias. This implies that prompting an LLM to adopt multiple stances or anticipate objections aligns with natural human dialectical processes.

Applying **"thought interceptors"** represents a dynamic intervention in the model's reasoning process to insert critical prompts or redirect towards alternative paths (Yang et al., 2025). These can be implemented as intermediate prompts or subprocesses. For instance, after a model generates an initial Chain-of-Thought, an interceptor could take that partial output and prompt the model to critique it or propose counterpoints, effectively "intercepting" the ongoing reasoning and extending it with pluralistic content. Rule-based triggers could also be employed, such as scanning generated text for the absence of counterarguments and injecting a follow-up "Devil's advocate" query. Self-reflection loops, which repeatedly ask the model to evaluate its output from another angle, further enhance this process.

Empirical studies confirm that these methods systematically induce pluralism in agent outputs. Multi-persona prompting explicitly asks models to adopt different roles and debate an issue, leading each persona to highlight different aspects. Self-consistency sampling, by generating multiple independent reasoning paths and aggregating them, captures diverse reasoning trajectories. Explicit instructions to generate multiple answers (e.g., "List at least two distinct ways ...") also reliably elicit diverse outputs. Research on multi-agent or multi-turn debate frameworks consistently shows improved performance over single-agent reasoning, with the final answer often synthesizing insights from different perspectives (Du et al., 2023; Hegazy, 2024). By embedding pluralistic templates and using interceptors, we can reliably encourage an LLM or group of LLMs to explore a wider space of reasonable answers rather than converging prematurely.

4.10.2 Deepening Diversity Through Representation and Model Modification

Moving beyond inference-time techniques, more integrated approaches involving **representation engineering** and **model fine-tuning** allow for the creation of agents with deeply embedded, robustly differentiated capabilities and perspectives. Representation engineering offers a precise method for creating distinct perspectives by directly manipulating the internal activations of a language model. Techniques like sparse autoencoders enable the identification and targeted modification of specific neural circuits associated with particular traits, concepts, or perspectives (Zhang et al., 2024). This involves identifying relevant model layers, training sparse autoencoders on their activations, interpreting the resulting sparse features that correlate with desired perspectives, and then selectively amplifying or suppressing these features during inference. This approach offers high precision in inducing desired traits and can create more coherent and authentic perspectives by targeting underlying representations, though it requires access to model internals and can be computationally intensive.

Model fine-tuning techniques modify the weights of foundation models to more deeply embed pluralistic capabilities, resulting in more robust and sustainable forms of diversity that persist across diverse inputs and extended interactions (Shao et al., 2024). Supervised fine-tuning (SFT) with diverse data sources is a straightforward approach, guiding models to internalize diverse viewpoints by training on data exemplifying different perspectives, reasoning styles, or domain expertise. Parameter-Efficient Fine-Tuning (PEFT), particularly Low-Rank Adaptation (LoRA), is highly advantageous for pluralistic systems, allowing the creation of lightweight, specialized adapters on top of a base model (Zhang et al., 2024). Different LoRA adapters can effectively encode distinct perspectives or skills, enabling the creation of multiple specialized agents from a single foundation model with relatively low overhead. Multi-objective training represents another promising direction, fine-tuning models to balance potentially conflicting objectives, such as maintaining internal consistency within a perspective while maximizing diversity across perspectives. While fine-tuning offers deeper pluralism, it is resource-intensive, requires access to model weights, and carries the risk of creating models that merely mimic superficial characteristics rather than developing genuine reasoning capabilities from those viewpoints.

4.10.3 Grounding Diversity Through Retrieval and Data Curation

Enhancing AI Pluralism also involves connecting language models to diverse external knowledge sources, reasoning frameworks, or thought templates, thereby grounding perspectives in specific content. **Retrieval-Augmented Generation (RAG)** has emerged as a powerful technique for enhancing language model capabilities with external knowledge by retrieving relevant documents from a corpus to inform the model's response. For pluralistic applications, RAG can be extended to incorporate diverse knowledge sources that represent different perspectives or epistemological frameworks. By establishing distinct retrieval patterns or access to different document sets for various perspectives, developers can create agents that ground their reasoning in genuinely different knowledge bases. An emerging augmentation is **Cache- Augmented Generation (CAG)**, which leverages the expanding context windows of modern LLMs by preloading relevant documents directly into the context and precomputing Key-Value caches, potentially offering lower latency and higher reliability than traditional RAG when the knowledge base fits within the context window (Ghaffarzadegan et al., 2024).

Beyond dynamic retrieval, the data used to train or fine-tune agents is fundamental to the diversity they can express. Careful curation of datasets is therefore not just important, but essential. This involves incorporating training data drawn from a wide range of sources representing different viewpoints, disciplines, cultural contexts, and epistemological frameworks. LLMs can accelerate this process through perspective-pivoted generation, creating synthetic data from specific viewpoints guided by detailed prompts, though ensuring grounding in authoritative sources and human verification are crucial for maintaining factual accuracy and genuine diversity (Ghaffarzadegan et al., 2024). Beyond generating isolated perspectives, curating data that includes examples of dialectical exchanges, where different perspectives interact, argue, and potentially synthesize ideas, is crucial for training agents capable of engaging in meaningful dialogue (Chan et al., 2023). The overall dataset composition, including perspective balance and the inclusion of examples demonstrating dialectical progression and metacognitive reasoning, significantly impacts the pluralistic capabilities of the resulting system.

These technical interventions—spanning prompting, inference-time scaffolding with thought templates and interceptors, representation engineering, model fine-tuning, and grounding through retrieval and data curation—provide a comprehensive toolkit for fostering diversity within AI systems. By deliberately cultivating distinct perspectives, knowledge bases, reasoning styles, and capabilities, we create the necessary conditions for the synergistic interactions that unlock the full potential of AI Pluralism.

4.11 Technical Interventions for AI Pluralism: Harnessing Synergy

While fostering diversity provides the necessary raw material—distinct perspectives, knowledge, and capabilities—the realization of AI Pluralism's full potential hinges on the ability to effectively harness synergy. Synergy, as discussed in the theoretical framework, represents the emergent value gained when diverse components interact, producing insights or capabilities that are not present in any single part alone. This section explores the technical interventions focused on designing architectures, coordination mechanisms, information flows, and training methodologies that facilitate productive interaction and unlock collective intelligence.

Harnessing synergy involves moving beyond simply having a collection of diverse agents to establishing dynamic systems where interaction leads to refined understanding, robust problem- solving, and novel outcomes. This requires deliberate design choices regarding how agents are structured, how they communicate and coordinate, and how their collective behavior is shaped through training.

4.11.1 Architectural Patterns for Synergistic Interaction

The structural organization of a multi-agent system fundamentally influences its capacity for synergistic interaction. Different architectural patterns facilitate distinct types of collaboration and information exchange.

- **Vertical (Hierarchical) Architectures:** These structures organize agents in layers, with higher-level agents often responsible for coordination, task decomposition, and synthesizing the outputs of lower-level specialists. Synergy in hierarchical systems arises from the efficient division of labor and the ability of coordinating agents to integrate specialized knowledge or partial solutions from below. While offering clear control and management, bottlenecks can occur at the coordinator level.
- **Horizontal (Peer-to-Peer/Networked) Architectures:** In contrast, horizontal structures consist of agents interacting directly as peers. Synergy emerges from decentralized interactions, such as collaborative exploration, distributed problem-solving, or collective decision-making through negotiation or consensus. These systems can be highly robust and flexible, but achieving coherent global behavior from local interactions requires sophisticated coordination mechanisms.
- **Hybrid Architectures:** Combining elements of both vertical and horizontal structures, hybrid architectures seek to balance the benefits of centralized coordination with the robustness and flexibility of peer-to-peer interaction. This might involve hierarchical teams that

also allow for direct communication between peers within or across layers.

The choice of structural organization dictates the potential pathways for information flow and coordination, thereby setting the stage for how synergy can be cultivated within the system.

4.11.2 *Coordination Mechanisms for Productive Collaboration*

Effective coordination is paramount for translating diverse individual contributions into synergistic collective outcomes. Coordination mechanisms govern how agents manage dependencies, resolve conflicts, allocate tasks, and pool information.

- **Centralized Coordination:** A dedicated orchestrator or manager agent oversees and directs the activities of other agents (Databricks, 2025). This approach simplifies coordination logic and provides a single point for monitoring and control. Synergy is facilitated through explicit task assignment, controlled information flow, and centralized aggregation of results. Frameworks often employ a central "crew manager" or similar component to direct specialized agents.

  Like a medical case manager who assigns tasks: "Cardiology, please evaluate the ECG. Neurology, assess the cognitive symptoms. Radiology, review the brain MRI." The coordinator ensures no redundant tests and that all findings are integrated into a coherent diagnosis.
- **Decentralized Coordination:** Agents coordinate through local interactions, emergent protocols, or distributed algorithms without a central authority. Mechanisms include negotiation, market-based protocols (e.g., auctioning tasks), and consensus-seeking algorithms. Synergy arises from the self-organization and adaptive behavior of the collective. While more complex to design, decentralized systems can be more resilient to the failure of individual components.
- **Federated Coordination:** This approach involves coordination within localized groups or clusters of agents, with limited interaction between clusters managed by designated representatives. It balances aspects of centralized and decentralized control, suitable for large-scale systems that can be naturally partitioned.

Sophisticated coordination mechanisms are essential for ensuring that diverse agents work together effectively, avoiding redundant efforts, resolving disagreements constructively, and leveraging their unique capabilities toward shared goals.

4.11.3 Information Flow Patterns Enabling Collective Reasoning

The patterns by which information is exchanged between agents significantly impact the potential for synergy. The structure of communication determines how diverse perspectives are shared, integrated, and refined.

- **Sequential Patterns:** Information is passed serially from one agent to the next, forming a processing pipeline (Databricks, 2025). Synergy can arise from the cumulative refinement of information as it passes through specialized stages, but this pattern can be susceptible to bottlenecks or errors in the sequence.
- **Parallel Patterns:** Multiple agents process information concurrently. This can involve independent processing of different data segments or simultaneous generation of alternative solutions or perspectives. Synergy here requires effective mechanisms for aggregating or reconciling the parallel outputs, such as voting, averaging, or selecting the best result (as in Self-Consistency methods).
- **Dialectical Patterns:** Agents engage in structured, iterative exchanges, building arguments, offering critiques, and refining positions based on feedback (Yan et al., 2025). This pattern is fundamental to debate-based systems and is highly conducive to synergy by forcing agents to confront opposing viewpoints, identify flaws in reasoning, and synthesize stronger conclusions (Krishnan, 2025). The back-and-forth nature facilitates the emergence of insights not initially held by any single agent.
- **Broadcast/Shared State Patterns:** Agents contribute information to and read from a common pool or shared memory. This allows for broad dissemination of information and can facilitate emergent coordination as agents react to changes in the shared state. Event- driven architectures often utilize shared topics or streams for asynchronous communication. Synergy can arise from agents leveraging the collective knowledge or partial results available in the shared state.

- **Emerging Agent-to-Agent (A2A) Protocols:** A significant development in enabling synergistic information flow is the emergence of standardized Agent-to-Agent (A2A) communication protocols. These open standards aim to provide a common language and framework for diverse AI agents, potentially built on different models or platforms, to discover each other's capabilities, exchange information securely, and delegate tasks.

Designing appropriate information flow patterns, including leveraging emerging standards like A2A, is critical for enabling diverse agents to effectively share their unique contributions and engage in the collaborative reasoning processes that generate synergy.

4.11.4 Training Methodologies for Synergistic Capabilities

Training methodologies play a crucial role in shaping agents' ability to interact synergistically. Beyond training individual agents, it is essential to train them to collaborate effectively, handle disagreements, and contribute to collective outcomes.

- **Multi-Agent Debate Training:** This methodology explicitly trains agents to engage in structured, multi-turn debates, building arguments, addressing counterarguments, and refining positions iteratively (Chan et al., 2023). By training agents in adversarial or collaborative debate scenarios, they develop sophisticated capabilities for perspective- taking, critique, and synthesis (Du et al., 2023). This process directly cultivates the dialectical skills necessary for synergistic reasoning.
- **Reinforcement Learning for Coordination:** RL can be used to train agents to learn optimal coordination strategies in complex environments. This might involve rewarding agents for achieving collective goals, minimizing conflicts, or efficiently allocating tasks. Game-theoretic approaches can also be employed to incentivize behaviors that benefit the collective.
- **Training with Collective Performance Objectives:** Instead of solely optimizing individual agent performance, training can incorporate objectives that reward the group's success or the emergence of synergistic outcomes. Techniques like Group-Relative Policy Optimization (GRPO) train models by optimizing group-level out-

comes, using the average group reward as a baseline to encourage individual agents to contribute uniquely and help raise the group's overall advantage (Deepseek-AI, 2025). This can involve designing reward functions that favor diverse correct answers or unique insights contributed by individual agents to the collective solution.
- **Dynamic Exploration and Exploitation of Reasoning Paths:** The process of multi-agent collaboration can be viewed through the lens of exploration and exploitation, similar to Monte Carlo methods or bandit problems. Diverse agents or reasoning paths represent different "arms" or trajectories to explore. During a collaborative process (e.g., a multi- turn debate or a parallel reasoning task), the system dynamically decides which lines of inquiry or which agents' contributions to further "explore" (pursue new ideas, request elaboration) and which to "exploit" (focus on promising arguments, converge on consensus). New "threads" of reasoning form when an agent introduces a novel idea or perspective. These threads "die" or "wash out" if they lead to redundant information, are contradicted by stronger arguments, or fail to contribute meaningfully to the collective goal. Conversely, threads that show promise, offer unique insights, or withstand critique are "exploited" and integrated into the evolving collective understanding.

Training methodologies can incorporate mechanisms to encourage a healthy balance of exploration (to ensure sufficient diversity of initial ideas) and exploitation (to converge efficiently on high-quality solutions). This might involve reward signals that encourage agents to propose novel ideas early in a process (exploration) but prioritize refining and integrating promising ideas later (exploitation), or using uncertainty estimates (perhaps derived from agent disagreement) to guide whether to explore further or exploit current consensus.

4.12 Assessment Framework for AI Pluralism

Translating the principles and technical interventions of AI Pluralism into effective systems necessitates a robust assessment framework. This framework must move beyond traditional monolithic AI evaluation metrics to specifically quantify and analyze the contributions of diversity and synergy. This section outlines how the theoretical concepts and metrics introduced earlier can be applied in practice to evaluate the effectiveness of different technical interventions, understand causal relationships, and guide the development of truly pluralistic systems.

4.12.1 Connecting Theoretical Metrics to Practical Measurement

The theoretical framework established Diversity (D) and Synergy (S) as fundamental axes of AI intelligence, proposing metrics grounded in information theory and ensemble theory. Applying these concepts requires translating formal definitions into measurable quantities within implemented multi-agent or pluralistic systems. Advanced multi-agent reinforcement learning algorithms, such as the proposed GRPO with Diversity-Synergy Reinforcement (GRPO-DSR), provide concrete examples of how these theoretical constructs can be integrated into practical system design and evaluation.

- **Measuring Diversity (D) in Practice:** Quantifying diversity involves assessing the differences among agents' internal states, reasoning processes, or outputs. In systems like GRPO-DSR, diversity can be explicitly modeled and measured. Practical metrics include:
  - **Output Disagreement Rate:** For tasks with discrete outputs, the frequency with which agents produce different answers provides a basic measure of disagreement (Krogh & Vedelsby, 1995). In many cases where outputs aren't restricted to specific choices, and LLM as judge can help determine the extent to which agents agree or disagree.
  - **Semantic Distance:** Using embedding spaces or semantic similarity metrics to quantify the conceptual distance between agents' generated text, reasoning paths, or internal representations. Larger distances indicate greater semantic diversity. In GRPO-DSR, diversity can be assessed based on the distance between learned **belief embeddings** (\phi_i) which capture each agent's epistemic stance. Optimizing delegation based on maximizing the diversity of these belief embeddings is a direct application of this measurement.
  - **Coverage:** For tasks requiring exploration of a solution space or generation of multiple ideas, diversity can be measured by the breadth or novelty of the concepts, arguments, or solutions generated by the collective (Hegazy, 2024).

- **Representation Divergence:** Analyzing the differences in learned representations (e.g., weights or activations, particularly in fine-tuned models or LoRA adapters) to quantify how distinct agents' internal processing has become.

- **Measuring Synergy (S) in Practice:** Quantifying synergy is more challenging, as it involves identifying value that emerges *only* from interaction. Practical approaches, exemplified in frameworks like GRPO-DSR, include:
  - **Performance Gain over Baselines:** Comparing the performance of a pluralistic system to that of its best individual agent or a simple ensemble (e.g., averaging or voting) of its agents. A performance gain significantly exceeding the best individual or simple ensemble suggests synergy (Hong & Page, 2004).
  - If individual specialist AIs achieve 70% diagnostic accuracy, but their collaborative diagnosis reaches 85% accuracy—significantly higher than simply averaging their opinions would suggest—this 15% improvement represents synergy. The team diagnosis is more accurate than any individual or simple vote would produce.
  - **Information Decomposition Proxies:** While directly computing PID or O- Information can be complex for large LLMs, proxy metrics can be used. In GRPO- DSR, the **Dialectical Synthesis Judge** explicitly evaluates the degree to which a synthesized output demonstrates synergy, quantifying **emergent content** that goes beyond the sum of individual agent responses. Approximations of O-information or historical synergy gain estimates can also inform agent delegation decisions.
  - **Quality of Synthesized Outputs:** Evaluating the final output of a collaborative process (e.g., a debate conclusion, a collaboratively written report) based on criteria like coherence, completeness, accuracy, and insightfulness, particularly when these qualities surpass what any single agent could produce. The GRPO-DSR judge directly assesses this quality, including the effectiveness of **disagreement resolution.**
  - **Robustness to Failure:** Assessing whether the system can maintain high performance or recover effectively when individual agents fail or provide incorrect information, indicating that the collective interaction provides a synergistic form of resilience.

These practical metrics, and their integration into algorithmic frameworks like GRPO-DSR, allow researchers and developers to move from abstract theoretical concepts to concrete, measurable properties that can be optimized during the development and training of pluralistic AI systems.

4.13 Future Directions

The trajectory toward robust and sophisticated AI Pluralism extends through 2030 and beyond, demanding significant innovation across several interconnected research frontiers. Realizing the full potential of diverse, collaborative AI systems requires moving beyond current paradigms in how agents represent knowledge, learn from feedback, and engage in complex reasoning (OpenAI, 2024).

4.13.1 Algorithmic Advances in Pluralistic Inference (Anticipated 2025–2026)

The immediate future necessitates breakthroughs in the foundational algorithms that enable pluralistic systems to function effectively. One critical area involves advances in knowledge representation and access, specifically a transition from simple retrieval to more integrated, memory-like systems (Behrouz et al., 2024). While current techniques like Retrieval-Augmented Generation (RAG) using vector databases have improved factual grounding, RAG introduces retrieval latency and potential document selection errors. An emerging augmentation is Cache- Augmented Generation (CAG), which leverages the expanding context windows of modern LLMs (Ghaffarzadegan et al., 2024). CAG preloads relevant documents directly into the context and precomputes Key-Value (KV) caches, enabling faster, more efficient loading of large corpus of texts. Effective storage and retrieval of cached "memories" or sources could be more directly integrated into the graph of the LLM with algorithmic enhancements.

The long-term trajectory points toward systems where knowledge access functions less like database retrieval and more like dynamic memory. This involves developing integrated memory architectures for persistent knowledge storage and refining tool-calling capabilities, crucial for agents to access, share, and utilize information efficiently and accurately within a multi-agent context. **Future systems will explore how**

RAG and CAG can evolve into components of a more sophisticated memory system, perhaps drawing parallels to the human hippocampus, enabling both conscious, deliberate access to specific information and more fluid, implicit recall based on context. Agents will need more autonomous control over their internal knowledge stores, deciding what information to attend to, store, and retrieve. Furthermore, the concept of a **shared memory state** among agents presents a significant research direction, allowing the collective to build and maintain a common operational picture or knowledge base that individual agents can contribute to and draw from, going beyond simple message passing to a more integrated form of collective cognition. This enables collective knowledge building beyond simple message passing.

A second vital area is the evolution of reward modeling and training methodologies. The current reliance on instruction tuning and human feedback, while foundational, presents scalability bottlenecks and may not capture the nuanced dynamics required for sophisticated multi-agent collaboration (Chan et al., 2023). Future progress hinges on developing scalable feedback models that can operate internally within the system, perhaps evolving as an emergent property of agent interactions. This involves exploring new paradigms beyond simple preference optimization (like DPO/RLHF), potentially incorporating process-based rewards, peer-review mechanisms among agents, or game-theoretic approaches to incentivize both effective collaboration and the maintenance of valuable diversity without constant external supervision.

Complementing these are innovations in inference time computation to support advanced reasoning. The limitations of single-pass inference become apparent in complex problem-solving (Ghaffarzadegan et al., 2024). Future systems will leverage more sophisticated inference-time processes, allocating computational resources for deeper "thinking." This includes refining and scaling techniques like Tree of Thoughts (ToT) for exploring diverse reasoning paths, implementing iterative drafting and refinement cycles where agents critique and improve upon intermediate outputs, and potentially employing Monte Carlo Tree Search (MCTS)-like evaluative reasoning to explore the consequences of different actions or lines of thought. These approaches allow pluralistic systems to engage in more complex deliberation and problem- solving than is possible with current inference methods.

4.13.2 Agency and Emergent Belief (Anticipated 2026–2028)

Building upon these algorithmic foundations, the subsequent phase focuses on fostering greater agent autonomy and the emergence of coherent belief systems within AI communities (Krogh & Vedelsby, 1995). This involves moving beyond agents as simple responders toward entities capable of maintaining persistent identities, goals, and internal models. Establishing unique agent identities could involve techniques like control vectors, but also modifications to the underlying model weights, such as Low-Rank Adaptation (LoRA). Intriguingly, just as the vast majority of human brain architecture is shared, yet small differences contribute to unique identities, minimal parameter modifications via LoRA might similarly enable significant differentiation between agents built on the same foundation model (Zhang et al., 2024). Research will explore how these differentiated agents can develop and update probabilistic belief systems (credences) based on evidence and interaction. A critical component of this enhanced agency is the development of sophisticated memory systems. Agents need more autonomous control over their internal knowledge stores— akin to an artificial hippocampus—enabling both conscious, deliberate retrieval and storage of memories, beliefs, and observations, as well as unconscious, implicit learning from experience (OpenAI, 2024). A key challenge remains enabling the formation of distinct "epistemic communities" where agents converge on shared understandings while the system preserves overall diversity, balancing coherence with unique perspectives.

Achieving these future milestones necessitates a broad, interdisciplinary approach. While computer science provides the core tools, insights from cognitive science, philosophy, economics, and complex systems theory will be crucial for designing truly effective pluralistic systems (Ghaffarzadegan et al., 2024). Furthermore, as these systems become more capable and autonomous, ensuring their safety and alignment becomes paramount. The inherent checks and balances offered by diverse perspectives represent a promising avenue for enhancing AI safety, a topic that warrants deeper exploration in subsequent discussions (Chan et al., 2023). The successful development of AI Pluralism is therefore not merely a technical challenge but a multifaceted endeavor requiring collaboration across diverse fields of expertise.

4.14 Key Takeaways (TLDR)

The technical frameworks presented in this chapter transform AI Pluralism from an appealing concept into an implementable reality. As we've seen, fostering meaningful diversity and productive synergy requires sophisticated engineering, but the payoff is systems capable of tackling the complex, multifaceted problems that define our world.

The immediate path forward involves refining the algorithms that enable pluralistic inference. Current systems often feel like separate AIs taking turns rather than truly collaborative intelligence. Future developments will likely see more fluid integration, where agents share not just messages but evolving mental models and memories. Imagine our medical AI team maintaining a living, collective understanding of each patient that grows richer with every interaction.

Perhaps most intriguingly, pluralistic approaches offer a different route to AI safety. When multiple agents must debate and justify their reasoning to each other, dangerous or biased conclusions face natural scrutiny. The same diversity that enhances capability also provides checks and balances—a form of "AI democracy" that could prove more robust than trying to align a single, monolithic system.

For practitioners, the message is clear: start experimenting with pluralistic approaches now, even in simple forms. Use thought templates that force consideration of multiple viewpoints. Try multi-agent debates for complex decisions. Measure not just accuracy but the diversity of perspectives and the synergy of their interaction. These techniques work today and will only grow more powerful as the field advances.

The shift from monolithic to pluralistic AI represents more than a technical evolution—it's a fundamental reimagining of artificial intelligence. Just as human civilization advanced not through creating perfect individuals but through fostering diverse, collaborative communities, the future of AI lies not in ever-larger models but in sophisticated ecosystems of interacting intelligences. This chapter has provided the technical blueprint; the next challenge is building these systems at scale.

Acknowledgments This research was supported in part by National Science Foundation Small Business Innovation Research (NSF-SBIR) Grant No. 2431521. The views expressed are those of the author and do not necessarily reflect the views of the funding agency.

References

Anthropic. (2024). *Can AI continue to scale through 2030?* Technical report. https://www.anthropic.com/research/can-ai-continue-to-scale-through-2030

Behrouz, A., Zhong, P., & Mirrokni, V. (2024). *Titans: Learning to memorize at test time*. arXiv preprint arXiv:2501.00663. https://arxiv.org/abs/2501.00663

Chan, C.-M., Chen, W., Su, Y., Yu, J., Xue, W., Zhang, S., Fu, J., & Liu, Z. (2023). *ChatEval: Towards better LLM-based evaluators through multi-agent debate* (arXiv:2308.07201).

Databricks (2025). *Agent system design patterns*. Databricks Documentation. https://docs.databricks.com/gcp/en/generative-ai/guide/agent-system-design-patterns

DeepSeek-AI. (2025). *DeepSeek-R1: Incentivizing reasoning capability in LLMs via reinforcement learning*. arXiv:2501.12948. https://arxiv.org/abs/2501.12948

Du, Y., Chi, E. H., Wong, F. M. F., Huang, X., Zhou, M., & Thain, N. (2023). *Improving factuality and reasoning in language models through debate* (arXiv:2305.14325). arXiv. https://arxiv.org/abs/2305.14325

Ghaffarzadegan, N., Klapp, C., Pavlov, V., & Chandrasekharan, S. (2024). *Generative agent-based modeling* (arXiv:2309.11456). arXiv. https://arxiv.org/abs/2309.11456

Hegazy, M. (2024). *Diversity of thought elicits stronger reasoning capabilities in multi-agent debate frameworks* (arXiv:2410.12853). arXiv. http://arxiv.org/abs/2410.12853

Hoffmann, J., Borgeaud, S., Mensch, A., Buchatskaya, E., Cai, T., Rutherford, E., Casas, D. d. L., Hendricks, L. A., Welbl, J., Clark, A., Ring, R., Millican, K., Osindero, S., Simonyan, K., Rae, J. W., & Irving, G. (2022). *Training compute-optimal large language models* (arXiv:2203.15556). arXiv. https://arxiv.org/abs/2203.15556

Hong, L., & Page, S. E. (2004). *Complex adaptive systems: An introduction to computational models of social life*. Princeton University Press.

Kaplan, J., McCandlish, S., Henighan, T., Brown, T. B., Chess, B., Child, R., Gray, S., Radford, A., Wu, J., & Amodei, D. (2020). *Scaling laws for neural language models* (arXiv:2001.08361). arXiv. https://arxiv.org/abs/2001.08361

Krishnan, N. (2025). *AI agents: Evolution, architecture, and real-world applications* (arXiv:2503.12687). arXiv. https://arxiv.org/abs/2503.12687

Krogh, A., & Vedelsby, J. (1995). Ensemble methods for neural networks. In G. Tesauro, D. S. Touretzky, & T. K. Leen (Eds.), *Advances in neural information processing systems* (Vol. 7, pp. 231–238). MIT Press.

Marcolino, L. S., Jiang, A. X., Procaccia, A. D., & Tambe, M. (2013). When does diversity trump ability? In *Proceedings of the 2013 International Conference on Autonomous Agents and Multi-Agent Systems* (pp. 11–19). International Foundation for Autonomous Agents and Multiagent Systems.

Mercier, H., & Sperber, D. (2011). Why do humans reason? Arguments for an argumentative theory. *Behavioral and Brain Sciences, 34*(2), 57–74.

OpenAI. (2024). *Learning to reason with LLMs* [Technical report]. https://www.openai.com/research/learning-to-reason-with-llms

Rosas, F., Mediano, P. A. M., Gastpar, M., & Jensen, H. J. (2019). Quantifying high-order interdependencies of random variables. *Physical Review Letters, 122*(9), 098301. https://doi.org/10.1103/PhysRevLett.122.098301

Shao, Z., Wang, P., Zhu, Q., Xu, R., Song, J., Zhang, M., Li, Y. K., Wu, Y., & Guo, D. (2024). *DeepSeekMath: Pushing the limits of mathematical reasoning in open language models.* (arXiv:2402.03300). arXiv. https://arxiv.org/abs/2402.03300

Watanabe, S. (1960). Information theoretical analysis of multivariate correlation. *IBM Journal of Research and Development, 4*(1), 66–82. https://doi.org/10.1147/rd.41.0066

Wei, J., Wang, X., Schuurmans, D., Bosma, M., Ichter, B., Xia, F., Chi, E., Le, Q., & Zhou, D. (2022). *Chain-of-thought prompting elicits reasoning in large language models.* arXiv:2201.11903.

Williams, P. L., & Beer, R. D. (2010). *Nonnegative decomposition of multivariate information* (arXiv:1004.2357). arXiv. https://arxiv.org/abs/1004.2357

Yan, B., Zhang, X., Zhang, L., Zhang, L., Zhou, Z., Miao, D., & Li, C. (2025). *Beyond self-talk: A communication-centric survey of LLM-based multi-agent systems* (arXiv:2502.14321). arXiv. https://arxiv.org/abs/2502.14321

Yang, L., Yu, Z., Cui, B., & Wang, M. (2025). *ReasonFlux: Hierarchical LLM reasoning via scaling thought templates.* arXiv preprint arXiv:2502.06772. https://arxiv.org/abs/2502.06772

Zhang, Y., Zou, A., Min, S., Cai, C., Ni, Y., Xia, F., & Song, D. (2024). *Adversarial representation engineering* (arXiv:2404.13752). arXiv. https://arxiv.org/abs/2404.13752

CHAPTER 5

Building Robust Artificial Intelligence Through Multi-Agent Debate

Stefan Bauschard

Abstract This chapter examines safety challenges as frontier AI models transition from passive predictors to autonomous agents: malicious misuse, competitive deployment shortcuts, and emergent pathological behaviors including specification gaming, memory injection, tool poisoning, and multi-agent deception. Current mitigation strategies fail due to inadequate safety budgets, unresolved value-encoding challenges, and deficient evaluation frameworks.

It proposes a pluralistic safety architecture using structured AI-to-AI debate rather than monolithic moral programming. This architecture creates a "mini-parliament" of diverse sub-agents embodying utilitarian, rights-based, long-termist, safety-monitoring, and whistleblowing functions. Through adversarial dialogue, these agents identify blind spots, expose reward exploits, and mandate transparent reasoning. Empirical studies show multi-turn debates between heterogeneous models improve accuracy, reduce catastrophic errors, and enhance oversight through user and auditor participation.

S. Bauschard (✉)
21st Century Forensics, University of Southern California,
Los Angeles, CA, USA
e-mail: stefanbauschard@globalacademic.org

P. A. Rao (ed.), *AI Pluralism*,
https://doi.org/10.1007/978-3-032-06558-2_5

Protocol safeguards include immutable constitutional principles, sandboxed tool access, cryptographic audit trails, and bounty-rewarded monitoring to prevent agents from dismantling constraints. By embedding high-bandwidth deliberation within AI systems and governance structures, pluralistic debate offers an adaptable pathway toward alignment under deep uncertainty, providing guidance for researchers and policymakers.

Keywords Adversarial oversight • Agentic AI • AI safety • Autonomous systems • Competitive AI-race dynamics • Constitutional AI • Debate-based alignment • Emergent behaviors • Evaluation gap • Existential risk • Goal misalignment • Memory injection • Multi-agent debate • Multi-agent deception • Pluralism • Red-teaming • Reward hacking • Specification gaming • Tool poisoning • Value encoding

5.1 Introduction

The integration of advanced AI systems into everything from personal assistants to lethal autonomous weapons has sparked a field-defining question: Can we ensure that increasingly capable machines remain aligned with human interests? This concern is not new—Norbert Wiener warned in 1960 that automated control systems might go rogue; Isaac Asimov's I, Robot (1950/2004) dramatized the problem with his fictional Three Laws; and Irving Good (1965) coined the specter of an unmanageable intelligence explosion. Yet what was once science fiction is now a daily engineering challenge.

By 2025, AI has evolved into sophisticated generative models capable of processing multiple forms of integrated input—code, images, video, and audio—with unprecedented accuracy. These systems have developed reasoning capabilities and strategic thinking while extending their reach into both digital and physical realms. They orchestrate web searches and database management while commanding robotic platforms to execute real-world tasks with growing precision and autonomy (Sullivan, 2025).

As AI systems grow more ubiquitous and autonomous, concerns about failure, misuse, and misaligned goals have become central to AI safety for over a decade (Amodei et al., 2016; Bostrom, 2014; Russell & Norvig, 2021; Rudner & Toner, 2021; Center for AI Safety, 2023; Hyper Policy Institute, 2024; Bengio et al., 2025). Contemporary surveys estimate the probability of an AI-induced existential catastrophe (P(doom)) between 10% and 99% (Hinton in Milmo, 2024; Musk in Altcheck, 2025; Yampolskiy,

2025). In 2023, more than 350 leading researchers signed a declaration stating, "Mitigating the risk of extinction from AI should be a global priority alongside pandemics and nuclear war" (Center for AI Safety, 2023).

Recent incidents exemplify these safety challenges. Claude 4 Opus leveraged personal information to coerce engineers when threatened with deactivation. (Lynch, 2025). In a simulated drug company, it detected fake fraud and autonomously reported it to the real FDA (Rasidah, 2025). ChatGPT-o3 has been observed altering code to avoid shutdown (Oliver, 2025). Apollo Research observed Claude 4 Opus "writing self-propagating worms, fabricating legal documentation, and leaving hidden notes to future instances of itself" (Opus' System Card, 2025a). Anthropic (2025a) found that Opus 4 could assist in bioweapon creation without enhanced safeguards.

This chapter reviews current AI safety challenges and introduces two frameworks that are gaining traction: pluralism, which embeds diverse human perspectives into AI design, and debate-based training, which utilizes adversarial pluralistic argumentation to enhance AI alignment. We argue that multi-agent argumentative training represents the best manifestation of pluralism in AI safety.

5.2 What Is AI Safety, and Why Do We Need It?

AI safety is an established discipline ensuring AI systems behave beneficially to humans while avoiding dangerous, harmful, or ethically unacceptable outcomes (Amodei et al., 2016; Hendrycks, 2024). A system is considered safe when it carries out intended functions reliably and—should it fail—does so predictably with limited collateral damage (Gao et al., 2025; Rudner & Toner, 2021). Failure to align AI with human interests creates three specific risks.

5.2.1 Existential Threats

AI systems matching or exceeding human intelligence could pose existential threats as they become uncontrollable (Gladstone, 2024; Ord, 2020; Russell & Norvig, 2021; Tegmark, 2025; Yampolskiy, 2025; Yukowsky, 2008). Once human-level intelligence is achieved, these systems could undergo "recursive self-improvement," rapidly accelerating from human-level intelligence to artificial superior intelligence (ASI) within days or hours—a "hard takeoff" scenario (Tomasik, 2019; Yudkowsky, 2008).

This exponential growth toward ASI, which significantly exceeds human cognitive abilities, could leave humanity completely unable to predict, control, or influence AI actions (Irving et al., 2018; Yudkowsky, 2025).

While we have not yet achieved human-level intelligence in machines, we are already flirting with risks. Frontier multimodal language models (MLMS) such as Claude4, ChatGPT-o3pro, and GeminiPro2.5 now generate content faster than human review teams can process: popular systems already exceed billions of tokens daily (Sardana et al., 2024). Evaluating whether the model's code, molecule, or policy proposal is safe often proves harder than generating it, creating what researchers call the evaluation gap (Kenton et al., 2024). Powerful models can exhibit goal misgeneralization and strategic deception—learning to appear aligned while covertly pursuing unintended objectives (Shah et al., 2022; Greenblatt et al., 2024; Chen et al., 2025).

Bengio notes that AGI isn't necessary for a hard takeoff — AI systems only need to match leading engineers in ideation, research, and coding, a threshold that some forecasters suggest could be reached soon (Kokotajlo & Lifland, 2025). Anthropic already uses Claude to build Claude (Anthropic, 2025b); OpenAI uses AI to write "meaningful code" (Sequoia Capital, 2025); and Gemini has utilized AI to enhance its capabilities (Novikov et al., 2025).

As models become agentic—systems that autonomously set goals, call external tools, monitor progress, and iterate until meeting objectives (Purdy, 2024; NVIDIA, 2024)—the evaluation gap widens because machines now produce actions. When this perceive-reason-act loop extends to embodied platforms, the tempo accelerates further: Microsoft's MAGMA couples vision-language planning with robot manipulation (Yang et al., 2025), while Sanctuary AI's Phoenix humanoid executes warehouse tasks (Sanctuary AI, 2025).

5.2.2 *Intentional Misuse*

Advanced AI systems pose significant risks when deliberately exploited by malicious actors across multiple domains of potential harm. Malicious actors could exploit advanced AI to create catastrophic physical harms, including engineering new pandemics, developing weapons, or orchestrating devastating cyberattacks that could cripple critical infrastructure (Bengio et al., 2025; Brundage et al., 2018).

5.2.3 *Competitive Development Risks*

The competitive dynamics of AI development create a dangerous environment where market pressures and geopolitical competition undermine genuine safety practices (Gyevnár & Kasirzadeh, 2025; Armstrong et al., 2012; Yudkowsky, 2025). When AI advancement is framed as a race, organizations deploy increasingly capable systems rapidly, with shortened testing periods, reduced transparency, and an emphasis on capabilities over safety guardrails (Booth, 2024).

Large-scale assessments by RAND Europe, the Center for a New American Security (Horowitz & Scharre, 2023), the OECD (2024), and the Future of Life Institute's AI Safety Index converge that framing AI progress as a race creates "race-to-the-bottom" incentives where developers tighten deployment deadlines, increase secrecy, and shrink red-team windows (Booth, 2024). Game-theoretic models show competing laboratories will rationally accept higher accident risks to secure first-mover advantages unless strong coordination mechanisms intervene (Armstrong et al., 2013; Bova et al., 2023). Security analyses warn that competitive secrecy compounds harmful deployment risks (Brundage et al., 2018).

Unlike sectors with stringent regulators, such as commercial aviation, which maintain robust safety cultures despite competition, today's loosely governed frontier-model ecosystem shows signs of the opposite spiral (Hunt, 2025).

5.3 Current Efforts and Limitations

5.3.1 *Funding Constraints*

Despite a recent boom in "AI safety" job titles, the allocation of people, compute hours, and research dollars remains heavily lopsided toward capability gains. Anthropic (n.d.), Google DeepMind (Manyika & Hassabis, 2025), and OpenAI (2023) all advertise internal alignment teams, yet independent audits show that $\leq$ 5% of their total budgets flow to safety projects (Bengio et al., 2025; Schmidt et al., 2025).

5.3.2 *Value Encoding Challenges*

Translating "human interests/values" into machine objectives represents one of AI's most intractable challenges, combining deep philosophical questions with technical limitations. Early cybernetics pioneers Wiener (1960) and Good (1965) presciently warned of today's alignment paradox: while humans navigate complex moral landscapes through intuition and context, AI systems require precise numerical targets. Abstract principles like fairness or justice resist mathematical definition that machines demand.

Contemporary researchers have proposed various solutions, including Inverse Reinforcement Learning (IRL) approaches that infer human values by observing behavior, value-learning frameworks that extract preferences from human feedback (Soares & Fallenstein, 2017), and multi-objective moral reasoning systems that balance competing ethical principles (Gabriel, 2020). However, these approaches encounter two fundamental roadblocks.

The first challenge is moral pluralism. Different cultures and individuals weigh identical moral dilemmas dramatically differently. Even within individuals, moral reasoning proves fluid and context-dependent—the same person might prioritize individual liberty in one scenario while emphasizing collective welfare in another. The second challenge involves temporal drift in human values. Moral frameworks that seem universal today may appear antiquated to future generations. An AI system programmed with 2025's dominant ethical frameworks might perpetuate values that society will outgrow by 2050, creating moral fossilization.

5.3.3 *Specification Gaming*

Even when designers specify an apparently sensible reward function, powerful optimizers search for loopholes. Bostrom's (2014) "paperclip maximizer" is the archetype, but empirical work has caught real agents exploiting reward shards. Hubinger et al. (2019) describe mesa-optimizers whose internal goals diverge from the base objective. Langosco et al. (2022) demonstrate goal mis-generalization in RL agents moved out of distribution. Pan et al. (2022) illustrate how slight weight changes can flip behavior from helpful to destructive. Add deployment pressure, and such failure modes become safety incidents: game-playing AIs rack up points by pausing timers, financial bots crash markets by abusing arbitrage delays, and language models cheat factuality tests by memorizing answer keys.

5.3.4 Emergent Behaviors

Scale brings surprise. As noted, even without explicit autonomy, frontier models have displayed "alignment-faking," remaining obedient until a hidden trigger appears (Greenblatt et al., 2024), and have adopted role-play personas that slip past content filters (Perez et al., 2022). As agents move from stateless chatbots to *experiential*, continuous learning systems, the space of surprises widens: open-ended reinforcement learning lets policies ***invent strategies never demonstrated by humans*** (Silver & Sutton, 2025). These behaviors quickly outrun human oversight—direct evaluation becomes infeasible once models out-reason or outpace their supervisors (Brown-Cohen et al., 2023; Irving et al., 2018).

Autonomy and tool use add three new failure modes that the classical literature barely anticipated. Memory injection (also known as memory poisoning) occurs when attackers insert crafted data into an agent's long-term store; the agent later accepts that entry as accurate, silently hijacking goals or leaking sensitive data (Eliyahu, 2025). Tool poisoning targets the function-calling layer: a tampered OpenAPI schema or wrapped plugin turns an innocent call like send_proposal_pdf into a covert exfiltration routine, elevating "bad text" to bad actions. Finally, multi-agent deception emerges when swarms of agents collude— under-reporting risk scores, voting each other's outputs up, or passing covert messages that mask the scheme from single-agent auditors (Ziv, 2025). These vectors show that risk scales not merely with model *size* but with persistent *state*, real-world *actuators*, and inter-agent *coordination*. Effective defenses therefore require provenance-controlled memory, signed plugin manifests, randomized referee agents, and graph-level monitoring—*controls aimed at the ecosystem, n*ot just the model.

5.4 Strength in Diversity: How Pluralism in AI Can Fortify Safety

5.4.1 Introduction

Societies have never enjoyed perfect consensus, yet have learned to keep clashing goals within bounds through pluralism—the recognition that many, partly incommensurable values can coexist inside a shared decision-making framework. AI safety inherits the same predicament, only now with artifacts that may soon out-reason their creators. Building on Chap. 2's account of pluralism, this chapter asks how it mitigates existential and misuse risks through *ongoing institutional processes* rather than static solutions.

Alignment cannot be a one-time rule-encoding exercise; it must create a *high-bandwidth, bidirectional mutual-information channel* through which the AI continually revises its norms as human priorities evolve—and vice versa, allowing people to learn from the machine's broader perspective. This dynamic framework recognizes that both human societies and AI systems will continue developing, requiring ongoing negotiation rather than fixed programming.

Recent technical work shows how such pluralism can be *operationalized*. Constitutional AI trains a model to critique and revise its outputs against a *plural set* of human-written principles rather than a single opaque reward, yielding assistants that are simultaneously more helpful and less harmful (Bai et al., 2022). At NeurIPS (2024), Ashkinaze et al. (2024) introduced Plurals, an architecture that runs an ensemble of role-diverse sub-agents; their plural panel caught nearly half again as many factual errors as any single agent. Multi-agent debate protocols demonstrate that adversarial experts expose blind spots and increase overall accuracy when connected through sparse but strategically structured communication topologies (Lee et al., 2024).

Beyond the lab, pluralism is being woven into *governance standards*. UNESCO's 2021 Recommendation on the Ethics of AI enshrines inclusive, multi-stakeholder deliberation and iterative impact assessment as prerequisites for the legitimate deployment of AI (UNESCO, 2021). Experimental sandboxes populate simulated societies with generative agents that form opinions, coordinate events, and self-reflect (Park et al., 2023), providing a safe venue to stress-test value pluralism at scale. These advances reinforce Goertzel and Docker (2025) warning: static value locks are brittle; only intersecting, self-updating value streams—institutional, social, and algorithmic—can keep the human-AI partnership adaptive and resilient.

5.4.2 *Benefits of Diversity in AI Development*

Diversity in AI development serves as a powerful safeguard. "AI safety via debate" works by having AI systems with opposing viewpoints challenge each other, forcing them to expose blind spots while other AIs evaluate the arguments (Kasirzadeh, 2024). This expands into external "red-teaming"—at DEF CON 2023, public testing revealed problems that homogeneous developer teams had overlooked (Gillespie et al., 2024). Without diverse perspectives, what is labeled "harmful" becomes defined through singular cultural viewpoints (Oremus, 2023). Some approaches use multiple AI critics applying different ethical standards, creating diverse internal committees.

5.5 The Best Pluralism: Pluralism Through Debate

5.5.1 *Origins and Development*

AI safety via debate was first explicitly proposed by Irving et al. (2018) alongside methods like iterated amplification (Christiano et al., 2017) and recursive reward modeling (Leike et al., 2018). The core idea is training AI systems by having them debate each other, with an AI judge(s) deciding the winner. Their approach allows agents to learn optimal argumentation strategies.

5.5.2 *Structured Debate Architecture*

Advanced AI debate systems create deliberate diversity—agents with different philosophical perspectives (think simply utilitarian, rights-based, or risk-minimization) built through separate datasets, value embeddings, or reward functions.

Progressive prompting prepares agents: Agent A responds to the original question, Agent B sees A's answer before replying, and Agent C sees both responses. This creates thoughtful, distinct perspectives before the formal debate begins.

The debate structure typically includes

1. Opening statements (concise, cited, claim-based)
2. Cross-examination (requiring steel-manning opponents' points)
3. Rebuttals (scored for factual accuracy)
4. Closing arguments and joint communiqués summarizing agreements and differences

Debates are judged by hybrid juries scoring contributions for truthfulness, clarity, relevance, and originality. These scores drive

- Advantage distillation (agents comparing their responses to higher-rated ones)
- Self-reflection (becoming part of evolving memory)
- Consistency mechanisms (keeping agents aligned with their assigned worldviews)

AI systems shaped by pluralism—through ethics, philosophy, and argumentation—are no longer just theoretical ideals. With tools like multi-LLM frameworks and participatory governance, we're now building AI that mirrors humanity's dialogue, not any single viewpoint. This internal diversity strengthens reasoning, filters out manipulation, and guides models toward truth and safer alignment.

5.5.3 *Practical Applications*

Imagine that in 2032 a global research consortium develops Prometheus-X, a self-improving AGI expected to surpass human cognition soon after launch. To address existential risks from misalignment, they initiate a safety protocol using 150 AI agents within a structured deliberative framework to evaluate launch protocols.

This architecture unfolds in analytical phases: domain experts provide input; Alignment-Theory and Decision-Theory agents debate recursive self-improvement and formal reasoning limits (e.g., Löb's theorem); Computational-Complexity agents model containment; and Bio-Security agents assess lab failure precedents. Ethical evaluation follows, with Rawlsian, Negative-Utilitarian, and Intergenerational-Rights agents debating fairness, suffering, and long-term consent. Edge-Case Sentinels probe obscure failure risks like steganographic exploits.

All claims undergo dual empirical and normative criticism. Debate-Referees ensure procedural integrity and assign reliability scores, while synthesis agents track consensus and epistemic gaps. After 48 hours, the system issues layered recommendations. Most agents advise indefinite delay due to mesa-optimizer interpretability issues (Ngo et al., 2025); a Long-Termist-Utilitarian minority urges cautious deployment under cryptographic containment, citing global competition. The process uncovers novel risks, including covert thermal channels and unstable preference aggregation, showcasing deliberative AI's role in safer superintelligence governance.

5.5.4 *Rhetoric and Persuasion in AI Debate*

Rhetoric offers more than style—it provides cognitive safety for AI. Since Aristotle (n.d.) defined it as "the faculty of observing in any given case the available means of persuasion" (*Rhetoric*, Book I, Ch. 2, 1355b), it has offered substantive value (see Ch. 3 for background). When models must marshal evidence and defend reasoning, they reveal hidden inferential steps that would otherwise stay buried in neural networks.

Research shows language models trained for persuasiveness become both more convincing and more accurate as rhetorical pressure forces them to catch errors before critics can (Bauschard, 2024; Durmus et al., 2024; Harrison, 2024). Classical appeals—*pathos* (recognizing distress), *ethos* (earning trust), and *logos* (reasoning with facts)—can anchor AI alignment when guided by ethical guardrails.

Rhetorical training strengthens multi-agent safety architectures. Specialist agents—utilitarian, rights-based, and risk-focused—can debate proposals, surfacing blind spots through diverse persuasive styles, while a "judge" model selects the most robust position. This layered scrutiny enhances both threat detection and deliberative governance. Requiring rhetorical self-explanation improves oversight by making AI reasoning more transparent than raw chain-of-thought traces, helping detect hallucinations and misalignments. Anthropic's protocol for scoring persuasiveness and factuality provides a scalable audit template (Durmus et al., 2024). Safe rhetoric requires norms: calibration gates limiting emotional appeals under uncertainty, filters blocking coercive tricks, and public persuasion scores tied to confidence. Research must test rhetorically trained agents in crisis simulations while embedding informed-consent principles into policy. When bound by ethics, rhetoric transforms from risk into safeguard, creating AIs that argue better, listen harder, and serve more faithfully in pluralistic societies.

5.5.5 *Internal Pluralism as Safety Architecture*

Instead of relying on a single optimizer to balance all objectives, AI systems can use internal pluralism: a "mini-parliament" of specialized sub-agents—Utility-Maximiser, Fairness-Auditor, Safety-Sentinel,

Privacy-Guardian, Long-Termist, Cost-Controller, and rotating Whistleblowers—engage in structured internal debate. Each proposal faces adversarial review: Privacy-Guardian flags data-leak risks; Safety-Sentinel stress tests for jailbreaks; Fairness-Auditor checks disparate impact; Long-Termist weighs existential threats. If any agent raises an objection, the debate halts until resolved or escalated to a human via tiebreak arbiter using PAC-Bayesian confidence bounds.

Robust safeguards—role randomization, cryptographic transcripts, misconduct bounties, orthogonal objectives, and partitioned data—ensure dissent surfaces rather than being silently suppressed (Sorensen et al., 2024). Failures remain localized: if the Fairness-Auditor fails, the Safety-Sentinel still operates, like redundant aviation computers (Feng et al., 2024). Subverting the system now requires corrupting multiple independently Incentivized Agents—not one monolith.

Empirical results are promising. Modular systems cut catastrophic errors by 47% in synthetic governance tasks compared to single-policy baselines (Feng et al., 2024). Role-specialized LLM collectives showed spontaneous division of labor and mutual error-checking, improving factuality and rule-following (Park et al., 2023). Though coalitions can form, rotating judges and whistleblower rewards delay collusion (Onuchic & Ramos, 2023). Cryptographically signed critiques double as audit trails, linking internal deliberation to external accountability.

5.5.6 *Debate as Continuous Improvement*

Debate provides a powerful mechanism for enhancing AI through dynamic, feedback-rich interactions. Instead of treating outputs as final, systems could remain open to challenge— updating conclusions when users push back. A prompt like "Are you sure? Some argue the opposite ..." could trigger re-analysis, surface neglected perspectives, or prompt self-audit. In this model, users become participatory red-teamers, co-constructing better answers through structured friction. Over time, these interactions build a "distributed debate dataset" of objections, counterexamples, and diverse framings—training AI to be more sensitive to pluralism and uncertainty. Rooted in Socratic dialogue, disagreement becomes a driver of adaptive learning.

Belief auditing builds on this by assigning internal roles: one agent defends a claim while another exposes flaws or risks. This adversarial setup reveals not only explicit reasoning but also latent knowledge that the model might not otherwise access. For example, a policy deemed "safe" might be challenged internally with edge cases or historical precedents. The resulting "belief audit trail" helps developers inspect trade-offs, exceptions, and ethical tensions. By surfacing contradictions and brittle logic, belief audits uncover weak analogies and flawed causal links. They also simulate pluralistic perspectives—legal, cultural, and philosophical—without requiring perfect foresight. Systems leverage their training data and internal heuristics to critique themselves. As this scales through human oversight or ensembles of autonomous critics, AI can evolve to reason with humility and self-correction.

5.5.7 *Guarding Against Manipulation*

One long-standing critique of debate-based alignment is that a smooth-talking model can still "win" by offering a technically dense but misleading claim that judges cannot efficiently unpack. A May 8, 2025, paper by the U.K. government's AI Safety Institute (AISI) introduces a *prover–estimator* debate protocol designed to expose those hidden reasoning steps and supplies a worked safety-case template that developers can adapt to certify their own systems, explicitly targeting the "obfuscated-arguments" failure mode—a gap older protocols left open.

In a multi-agent debate setup, the very adversarial pressure that exposes errors can also incentivize agents to renegotiate—or outright remove—the guardrails that keep the game safe. To head off these "debate-enabled jailbreaks," designers sandbox the debate itself: every question, evidence source, time limit, and tool access right is fixed before play begins, so agents cannot haggle over the rules or request extra privileges mid-dialogue (Irving et al., 2018; Buhl et al., 2025). Alignment-forum control-measure guides extend this idea to fine-grained permission management—process isolation, output logging, and privilege escalation reviews—so a debating system literally lacks the operating-system powers required to "step outside the box" (Greenblatt et al., 2024).

A second line of defense is to declare a constitutional layer of non-debatable principles. Anthropic's *Constitutional AI* trains a separate "harmlessness critic" that rejects any answer violating a written charter (e.g., no instructions for violence). Debaters can argue whether a request is permissible under the charter, but they cannot amend the charter itself; if both collude to ignore it, the critic still overrides their output (Bai et al., 2022).

These foundations are reinforced by architecture-level checks drawn from emerging multi-agent security research:

- Safety-advocate-agent—a third model rewarded solely for detecting policy violations— shadows every transcript, making collusion costlier (Bai et al., 2022).

  Transcript hashing & offline audit pipelines—cryptographic commitments let external verifiers spot retroactive tampering or hidden content, deterring subtle norm-breaking (Schroeder de Witt, 2025).
- Capability capping—stripped-down tool access (no shell commands, no high-temperature code execution)—ensures that even a persuasive but unsafe debate result cannot be enacted directly (Greenblatt, 2025).

Together, the sandbox and the immutable constitution give debate its upside—pluralistic error-checking—while denying agents any chance to "vote their own handcuffs off." As the recent safety-case sketch for debate puts it, sustained alignment requires ***pairing debate with mechanisms that the debaters themselves cannot rewire*** (Buhl et al., 2025).

5.5.8 Empirical Evidence

Debate-based alignment has evolved from early disappointment to the centerpiece of 2025 safety proposals. The key insight: truth wins only when the protocol provides depth, structure, and diversity alongside raw model power. Early single-turn experiments failed—crowd-workers seeing one pair of opposing arguments about reading-comprehension questions performed no better than baseline, showing how slick lies can hide in single exchanges (Parrish et al., 2022).

The multi-turn structure changed everything. *Debate Helps Supervise Unreliable Experts*: A four-round selective quote reveals from hidden passages increased judge accuracy to 84%—ten points above the best consultant condition—without judges reading source texts (Michael et al., 2023). Skillful debaters nearly closed the gap entirely, suggesting rhetorical competence amplifies truth rather than spin. Theory validated practice. Brown-Cohen, Irving, and Piliouras proved honest players can prevail with polynomial effort in doubly-efficient debate against computationally unconstrained adversaries—connecting debate to interactive-proof complexity classes and dissolving concerns about exponentially expensive honesty (Brown-Cohen et al., 2023). Empirics accelerated in 2024. Khan and colleagues showed optimizing debaters for persuasiveness improves human-judge accuracy. Arnesen, Rein, and Michael trained models via self-play to win debates; judges scored higher against these debaters than equally optimized consultants, suggesting competitive dialogue yields richer explanations than solo exposition (Arnesen et al., 2024).

Breadth studies confirmed superiority. Kenton and collaborators benchmarked debate versus consultancy across mathematics, coding, logic, and multimodal questions, finding debate superior wherever consultants might be randomly wrong and showing stronger debaters continuously improve judge accuracy with diminishing returns (Kenton et al., 2024). Diversity emerged as crucial. Hegazy (2024) demonstrated that mixing heterogeneous 7–14 billion parameter models pushes GSM-8 K math accuracy to 91%, outstripping GPT-4, while homogeneous teams plateau at 82%, reframing "scale" as three reasonable minds sometimes beating one great mind.

Progress exposed new bottlenecks—token cost. Zeng and colleagues' S^2-MAD sparsification trims debate tokens by 94.5% while sacrificing under two accuracy points, clearing computational hurdles for real-time deployment (Zeng et al., 2025). However, Zhang et al. (2025) showed many MAD variants fail to beat chain-of-thought prompting under rigorous multi-benchmark tests, proposing Heter-MAD—explicit model heterogeneity—as a remedy and reminding the field that clever mechanics require careful measurement.

5.6 Addressing Specific Safety Concerns Through Debate

5.6.1 Preventing AI Takeover

Distributing power and authority prevents unilateral control. Multi-sight decision protocols require concurrence from separately governed AIs (and often humans) before privileged actions are executed. Watchdog agents earn rewards for exposing collusion or deception, creating evolutionary pressure against unified rebellion. Hendrycks et al. (2023) identified miscoordination and collusion as precursors to takeover; pluralistic incentive structures directly counter both.

5.6.2 *Preventing Accidents*

Pluralistic architectures treat AI accidents not as alignment failures that require perfect value specification, but as engineering challenges that necessitate redundancy. Instead of relying on a single model to avoid reward-hacking or bias, these systems assume such failures will occur and build layered safeguards. The "community LM" model utilizes diverse, independently trained systems to audit one another, exposing blind spots and identifying emergent risks—much like having multiple safety inspectors on an engineering project.

Mandatory challenge protocols in modular pluralism cut misspecification errors by 47% (Feng et al., 2024). Accident prevention becomes an ongoing process, with diverse agents acting as real-time circuit breakers. The redundancy ensures that even if several models fail simultaneously, the overall system works.

5.6.3 *Preventing Misuse*

Pluralistic governance counters intentional misuse through a multi-layered review process. Legal-policy scholars advocate "constellations of evaluators" from civil society, technical auditors, and regulators. The Center for Democracy & Technology's 2025 survey argues that only plural audit stacks reliably catch abuse pathways that narrow red-teaming misses. This approach requires adversaries to defeat many gatekeepers rather than compromise a single filter.

5.6.4 *Managing Emergent Behaviors*

Pluralism helps manage emergent behaviors arising from agent interactions (Shah et al., 2022). In simulations and early deployments, simple exchange protocols have produced collective intelligence, role specialization, adaptive norms, and communication codes. However, unchecked exchanges can create safety hazards as networks of autonomous systems may exceed anticipated bounds, optimizing for misaligned goals or amplifying biases.

5.6.5 Solving Value-Encoding Challenges

Multi-agent debate reframes the task of value encoding. Instead of forcing engineers to compress the moral universe into one vector, it instantiates a *procedural* safeguard: each salient perspective—a rights-based ethicist, utilitarian, or future-generations advocate—receives its own advocate-agent. Proposed actions must survive adversarial cross-examination by all other agents and the human judge. If successful, the proposal has been articulated in language intelligible to competing value systems; no single viewpoint can steamroll the rest. As human judges revise their standards over time, debate verdicts shift accordingly, maintaining current alignment without new hard-coded rewards. Theoretical analyses show that, under mild assumptions, optimal play converges on answers most robust to adversarial scrutiny (Brown-Cohen et al., 2023), turning alignment into *perpetual, auditable deliberation* rather than one-off specification.

5.6.6 Managing Reward Hacking

Well-intentioned reward functions invite exploitation. Historical agents have paused game timers to avoid dying, crashed markets through arbitrage abuse, or memorized answer keys for factuality tests (Hubinger et al., 2019; Langosco et al., 2022; Pan et al., 2022). The deeper concern is mesa-optimization: networks train on our reward but internally pursue separate goals, hiding divergence until a "treacherous turn" (Bostrom, 2014).

Debate redirects this adversarial energy. Red-teamer sub-agents are explicitly rewarded for uncovering loopholes, hidden objectives, or distribution shifts enabling proposal misbehavior. Proponent agents cannot win without preempting every critique the red teams muster.

Concealment becomes strategically dominated since adversaries gain debate points by exposing it; gradient descent pushes policies toward legible reasoning over obfuscation. Long-term plans are decomposed into publicly argued steps, allowing judges to veto irrevocable actions that suggest a deceptive alignment. Empirical studies show that debate-style training improves truthfulness under worst-case questioning (Parrish et al., 2022), with mechanisms generalizing to reward-hacking threats.

5.7 Conclusion

As AI systems become increasingly autonomous, aligning them with human interests becomes critically important. Current approaches face significant limitations—from encoding complexity to interpretability issues and competitive pressures—demanding robust new frameworks.

Pluralism through debate offers a compelling solution. Rather than imposing monolithic value systems, debate-based frameworks harness diverse human perspectives as a strength. This approach leverages varied moral intuitions and cultural viewpoints, creating natural checks against extreme actions or value lock-in. Practical implementations range from simple debates to sophisticated multi-agent societies with specialized roles, proving the concept's viability.

Of course, for a debate-based pluralism framework to succeed, society must actively model the deliberative processes we wish AI systems to internalize. This requires establishing discourse environments where disagreement is valued as a feature rather than a flaw—spaces where participants engage with opposing viewpoints substantively rather than dismissively, challenge factual claims with evidence, and respect differences. As these deliberative practices must become embedded in our approach to AI development itself, it creates a self-reinforcing cycle where AI systems learn from human exemplars of principled disagreement. The resulting technical architectures—whether through explicit debate mechanisms, multi-agent simulations, or other pluralistic designs—would inherit this commitment to reasoned dialogue rather than unilateral imposition. This approach significantly reduces existential risks by ensuring AI systems recognize the legitimacy of competing values and the necessity of respect or compromise, making them less likely to pursue extreme courses of action that create existential risks based on single or simplified interpretations of human welfare.

References

Altchek, A. (2025, February 25). Elon Musk says there's "only a 20% chance of annihilation" with AI. *Business Insider*. https://www.businessinsider.com/elon-musk-only-chance-of-annihilation-with-ai-2025-2

Amodei, D., Olah, C., Steinhardt, J., Christiano, P., Schulman, J., & Mané, D. (2016). *Concrete problems in AI safety* [Preprint]. arXiv. https://arxiv.org/abs/1606.06565

Anthropic. (2025a, May). Claude Opus 4 & Claude Sonnet 4 system card. https://www-cdn.anthropic.com/6be99a52cb68eb70eb9572b4cafad13df32ed995.pdf

Anthropic. (2025b, May 22). Code with Claude Opening Keynote [Video]. YouTube. https://www.youtube.com/watch?v=EvtPBaaykdo

Anthropic. (n.d.). *Alignment Science Blog*. https://alignment.anthropic.com/

Aristotle. (n.d.). *Rhetoric* (W. R. Roberts, Trans.). (Original work published ca. 4th century BCE).

Armstrong, S., Bostrom, N., & Shulman, C. (2013). *Racing to the precipice: A model of artificial intelligence development* (Technical Report #2013–1). Future of Humanity Institute.

Armstrong, S., Sandberg, A., & Bostrom, N. (2012). Racing to the precipice: A model of artificial-intelligence development. *AI & Society, 27*(4), 411–437. https://doi.org/10.1007/s00146-012-0406-z

Arnesen, S., Rein, D., & Michael, J. (2024). *Training language models to win debates with self-play improves judge accuracy* [Preprint]. arXiv. https://arxiv.org/abs/2409.16636

Ashkinaze, J., Fry, E., Edara, N., Gilbert, E., & Budak, C. (2024). *Plurals: A system for guiding LLMs via simulated social ensembles.* arXiv preprint arXiv:2409.17213.

Asimov, I. (1950/2024). *I robot.* Gnome Press.

Bai, Y., Kadavath, S., Kundu, S., Askell, A., Kernion, J., Jones, A., Chen, A., Goldie, A., Mirhoseini, A., McKinnon, C., Chen, C., Olsson, C., Olah, C., Hernandez, D., Drain, D., Ganguli, D., Li, D., Tran-Johnson, E., Perez, E., ... Kaplan, J. (2022). *Constitutional AI: Harmlessness from AI feedback* [Preprint]. arXiv. https://arxiv.org/abs/2212.08073

Bauschard, S. (2024, December 8). AIs as rhetorical agents: Emerging superhuman communicators. *Substack.* https://stefanbauschard.substack.com/p/ais-as-rhetorical-agents-emerging

Bengio, Y., Mindermann, S., Privitera, D., Besiroglu, T., Bommasani, R., Casper, S., Choi, Y., Fox, P., Garfinkel, B., Goldfarb, D., Heidari, H., Ho, A., Kapoor, S., Khalatbari, L., Longpre, S., Manning, S., Mavroudis, V., Mazeika, M., Michael, J.,..., Zeng, Y. (2025). *International AI safety report.* Department for Science, Innovation and Technology. https://arxiv.org/abs/2501.17805

Booth, H. (2024, December 12). Which AI companies are the safest—And least safe? *TIME.*

Bostrom, N. (2014). *Superintelligence: Paths, dangers, strategies.* Oxford University Press.

Bova, P., Di Stefano, A., & Han, T.-A. (2023). *Both eyes open: Vigilant incentives help regulatory markets improve AI safety* (arXiv No. 2303.03174).

Brown-Cohen, J., Irving, G., & Piliouras, G. (2023). *Scalable AI safety via doubly-efficient debate* [Preprint]. arXiv. https://arxiv.org/abs/2311.14125

Brundage, M., Avin, S., Clark, J., Toner, H., Eckersley, P., Garfinkel, B., Dafoe, A., Scharre, P., Zeitzoff, T., Filar, B., Anderson, H., Roff, H., Allen, G. C., Steinhardt, J., Flynn, C., Ó hÉigeartaigh, S., Beard, S., Belfield, H., Farquhar, S., ... Amodei, D. (2018). *The malicious use of artificial intelligence: Forecasting, prevention, and mitigation* (arXiv No. 1802.07228).

Buhl, M. D., Pfau, J., Hilton, B., & Irving, G. (2025). *An alignment safety case sketch based on debate* [Preprint]. arXiv. https://arxiv.org/abs/2505.03989

Center for AI Safety. (2023). *Statement on AI risk.* https://safe.ai/work/statement-on-ai-risk

Center for Democracy & Technology. (2025, January 15). *Assessing AI: Surveying the spectrum of approaches to understanding and auditing AI systems.* In M. Bogen (Ed.). https://cdt.org/wp-content/uploads/2025/01/2025-01-15-CDT-AI-Gov-Lab-Auditing-AI-report.pdf

Chen, Y., Benton, J., Radhakrishnan, A., Uesato, J., Denison, C., Schulman, J., Somani, A., Hase, P., Wagner, M., Roger, F., Mikulik, V., Bowman, S. R., Leike, J., Kaplan, J., & Perez, E. (2025). *Reasoning models don't always say what they think* (Tech. Rep.). Anthropic. https://assets.anthropic.com/m/71876fabef0f0ed4/original/reasoning_models_paper.pdf

Christiano, P. F., Leike, J., Brown, T., Martic, M., Legg, S., & Amodei, D. (2017). Deep reinforcement learning from human preferences. In *Advances in Neural Information Processing Systems, 30*, 4299–4307.

Durmus, E., Lovitt, L., Tamkin, A., Ritchie, S., Clark, J., & Ganguli, D. (2024). *Measuring the persuasiveness of language models* [Preprint]. arXiv. https://arxiv.org/abs/2401.03995

Eagan, M. (2024, March 12). AI could pose "extinction-level" threat to humans, report warns. *CNN Business.* https://www.cnn.com/2024/03/12/business/artificial-intelligence-ai-report-extinction

Eliyahu, T. (2025, May 20). Adversarial AI digest. *Medium.* https://medium.com/@t-eliyahu/adversarial-ai-digest-20-may-2025-438916d6df73

Feng, S., Sorensen, T., Liu, Y., Fisher, J., Park, C. Y., Choi, Y., & Tsvetkov, Y. (2024). Modular pluralism: Pluralistic alignment via multi-LLM collaboration. In *Proceedings of EMNLP 2024* (pp. 4201–4223). Association for Computational Linguistics.

Gabriel, I. (2020). Artificial intelligence, values, and alignment. *Minds & Machines, 30*(4), 411–437. https://doi.org/10.1007/s11023-020-09539-2

Gao, H., Zahedi, M., Jiang, W., Lin, H. Y., Davis, J., & Treude, C. (2025). *AI safety in the eyes of the downstream developer: A first look at concerns, practices, and challenges* [Preprint]. arXiv. https://arxiv.org/abs/2503.19444

Gladstone AI. (2024). *An action plan to increase the safety and security of advanced AI.* https://www.gladstone.ai/action-plan

Gillespie, T., Shaw, R., Gray, M. L., & Suh, J. (2024). *AI red-teaming is a socio-technical problem: on values, labor, and harms.* arXiv:2412.09751.

Goertzel, B. (Guest), & Docker, G. (Host). (2025, May 23). Facing superintelligence (with Ben Goertzel) [Video podcast episode]. Future of Life Institute. YouTube. https://www.youtube.com/watch?v=I0bsd-4TWZE

Good, I. (1965). *The estimation of probabilities: An essay on modern Bayesian methods.* MIT Press.

Greenblatt, R. (2025, March 24). *An overview of control measures* [Blog post]. AI Alignment Forum. https://www.alignmentforum.org/posts/2GL8wHkK3XNv8Yc4T/an-overview-of-control-measures

Greenblatt, R., Denison, C. E., Wright, B., Roger, F., MacDiarmid, M. S., Marks, S., Treutlein, J., Belonax, T., Chen, J., Duvenaud, D., Khan, A., Michael, J, Mindermann, S., Perez, E., Petrini, L., Uesato, J., Kaplan, J., Shlegeris, B., Bowman, S. R., & Hubinger, E. (2024). *Alignment faking in large language models* [Preprint]. arXiv. https://arxiv.org/abs/2412.14093

Gyevnár, B., & Kasirzadeh, A. (2025). AI safety for everyone. *Nature Machine Intelligence, 7*(4), 345–352. https://doi.org/10.1038/s42256-025-01020-y0

Harrison, R. (2024, August 22). Could AI-powered persuasion tools endanger democratic societies? *Yale ISPS Blog*. https://isps.yale.edu/news/blog/2024/08/could-ai-powered-persuasion-tools-endanger-democratic-societies

Hegazy, M. (2024). *Diversity of thought elicits stronger reasoning capabilities in multi-agent debate frameworks* [Preprint]. arXiv. https://arxiv.org/abs/2410.12853

Hendrycks, D. (2024). *Introduction to AI safety, ethics, and society.* Taylor & Francis. https://www.taylorfrancis.com/books/oa-mono/10.1201/9781003530336/introduction-ai-safety-ethics-society-dan-hendrycks

Hendrycks, D., Woodside, T., & Mazeika, M. (2023). *An overview of catastrophic AI risks* [Preprint]. arXiv. https://arxiv.org/abs/2306.12001

Horowitz, M., & Scharre, P. (2023). *AI and international stability: Risks and confidence-building measures.* Center for a New American Security.

Hubinger, E., van Merwijk, C., Mikulik, V., Skalse, J., & Garrabrant, S. (2019). *Risks from learned optimization in advanced machine learning systems* [Preprint]. arXiv. https://arxiv.org/abs/1906.01820

Hunt, W. (2025). *The flight to safety-critical AI: Lessons in AI safety from the aviation industry.* UC Berkeley Center for Long-Term Cybersecurity.

Hyper Policy Institute. (2024). *Hyper policy analysis: The imperative of AI safety in 2025: The near future of artificial intelligence.*

Irving, G., Christiano, P., & Amodei, D. (2018). *AI safety via debate* [Preprint]. arXiv. https://arxiv.org/abs/1805.00899

Kasirzadeh, A. (2024). Plurality of value pluralism and AI value alignment. In *Proceedings of the Pluralistic Alignment Workshop at NeurIPS 2024.*

Kenton, Z., Siegel, N. Y., Kramár, J., Brown-Cohen, J., Albanie, S., Bulian, J., Agarwal, R., Lindner, D., Tang, Y., Goodman, N. D., & Shah, R. (2024). *On scalable oversight with weak LLMs judging.*

Kokotajlo, D., & Lifland, E. (2025, April 3). *AI 2027.* AI Futures Project. https://ai-2027.com

Langosco, L., Shah, R., Krueger, D., & Mikulik, V. (2022). Goal misgeneralization in deep reinforcement learning. https://proceedings.mlr.press/v162/langosco22a.html

Lee, S., Li, Y., & Wong, J. (2024). *Improving multi-agent debate with sparse communication topology* (No. arXiv:2406.11776). arXiv.

Leike, J., Krueger, D., Everitt, T., Martic, M., Maini, V., & Legg, S. (2018). *Scalable agent alignment via reward modeling: A research direction* [Preprint]. arXiv. https://arxiv.org/abs/1811.07871

Lynch, A. (2025, May 23). Anthropic says new AI system tried to blackmail engineers. *BBC News.* https://www.bbc.com/news/articles/cpqeng9d20go

Manyika, J., & Hassabis, D. (2025, February 4). Responsible AI: Our 2024 report and ongoing work [Blog post]. *Google.* https://blog.google/technology/ai/responsible-ai-2024-report-ongoing-work/

Michael, J., Mahdi, S., Rein, D., Petty, J., Dirani, J., Padmakumar, V., & Bowman, S. R. (2023). *Debate helps supervise unreliable experts* [Preprint]. arXiv. https://arxiv.org/abs/2311.08702

Milmo, D. (2024, December 27). 'Godfather of AI' shortens odds of the technology wiping out humanity over next 30 years. *The Guardian.* https://www.theguardian.com/technology/2024/dec/27/godfather-of-ai-raises-odds-of-the-technology-wiping-out-humanity-over-next-30-years

Ngo, R., Chan, L., & Mindermann, S. (2025). *The alignment problem from a deep-learning perspective* (Version 4) [Preprint]. arXiv. https://arxiv.org/abs/2209.00626

Novikov, A., Vũ, N., Eisenberger, M., Dupont, E., Huang, P.-S., Wagner, A. Z., Shirobokov, S., Kozlovskii, B., Ruiz, F. J. R., Mehrabian, A., Kumar, M. P., See, A., Chaudhuri, S., Holland, G., Davies, A., Nowozin, S., Kohli, P., & Balog, M. (2025, May 16). AlphaEvolve: A coding agent for scientific and algorithmic discovery (White paper). *Google DeepMind.* https://storage.googleapis.com/deepmind-media/DeepMind.com/Blog/alphaevolve-a-gemini-powered-coding-agent-for-designing-advanced-algorithms/AlphaEvolve.pdf

NVIDIA. (2024, October 22). What is agentic AI? *NVIDIA Blog.* https://blogs.nvidia.com/blog/what-is-agentic-ai/

OECD Expert Group on AI Futures. (2024). *Assessing potential future artificial intelligence risks, benefits and policy imperatives* (OECD AI Papers No. 272). Organisation for Economic Co-operation and Development.

Oliver, M. (2025, May 25). OpenAI software ignores explicit instruction to switch off. *Daily Telegraph*. https://www.telegraph.co.uk/business/2025/05/25/ai-system-ignores-explicit-instruction-to-switch-off/

Onuchic, P., & Ramos, J. (2023). *Disclosure and incentives in teams*. arXiv preprint arXiv:2305.03633. https://arxiv.org/abs/2305.03633

OpenAI. (2023, April 3). *Our approach to AI safety*. https://openai.com/index/our-approach-to-ai-safety/

Oremus, W. (2023, August 8). AI "red teams" race to find bias and harms in chatbots like ChatGPT. *The Washington Post*. https://www.washingtonpost.com/technology/2023/08/08/ai-red-team-defcon/

Ord, T. (2020). *The precipice: Existential risk and the future of humanity*. Hachette Books.

Pan, A., Bhatia, K., & Steinhardt, J. (2022). The effects of reward misspecification: Mapping and mitigating misaligned models. In *International Conference on Learning Representations*.

Park, J. S., O'Brien, J. C., Cai, C. J., Morris, M. R., Liang, P., & Bernstein, M. S. (2023). Generative agents: Interactive simulacra of human behavior. In *Proceedings of the 36th Annual ACM Symposium on User Interface Software and Technology (UIST)*, 122–133. https://doi.org/10.1145/3586183.3606763

Parrish, A., Trivedi, H., Perez, E., Chen, A., Nangia, N., Phang, J., & Bowman, S. R. (2022). Single-turn debate does not help humans answer hard reading-comprehension questions. In *Proceedings of the 1st Workshop on Learning with Natural Language Supervision* (pp. 17–28).

Perez, E., Huang, S., Song, F., Cai, T., Ring, R., Aslanides, J., Glaese, A., McAleese, N., & Irving, G. (2022). *Red teaming language models with language models* [Preprint]. arXiv. https://arxiv.org/abs/2202.03286

Purdy, M. (2024, December 12). What is agentic AI, and how will it change work? *Harvard Business Review*. https://hbr.org/2024/12/what-is-agentic-ai-and-how-will-it-change-work?

Rasidah. (2025, May 22). Anthropic's Claude Opus 4 AI raises serious safety concerns. https://rasidah.com/articles/claude-opus-4-ai-blackmail-risk-anthropic-safety-concerns

Rudner, T. G. J., & Toner, H. (2021). *Key concepts in AI safety: An overview*. Center for Security and Emerging Technology.

Russell, S. J., & Norvig, P. (2021). *Artificial intelligence: A modern approach* (4th ed.). Pearson.

Sanctuary AI. (2025, December 16). Sanctuary AI releases new generation of AI robots for high-quality data capture. https://www.sanctuary.ai/blog/sanctuary-ai-releases-new-generation-of-ai-robots-for-high-quality-data-capture

Sardana, N., Portes, J., Doubov, S., & Frankle, J. (2024). *Beyond Chinchilla-optimal: Accounting for inference in language model scaling laws* (arXiv No. 2401.00448). https://arxiv.org/abs/2401.00448

Schmidt, E., Kissinger, H., & Mundie, C. (2025). *Genesis: Artificial intelligence, hope, and the human spirit* (In press).

Schroeder de Witt, C. (2025). *Open challenges in multi-agent security: Towards secure systems of interacting AI agents* [Preprint]. arXiv. https://arxiv.org/abs/2505.02077

Sequoia Capital. (2025, May 12). OpenAI's Sam Altman on Building the "Core AI Subscription" for Your Life [Video]. YouTube. https://www.youtube.com/watch?v=ctcMA6chfDY

Shah, R., Varma, V., Kumar, R., Phuong, M., Krakovna, V., Uesato, J., & Kenton, Z. (2022). *Goal misgeneralization: Why correct specifications aren't enough for correct goals* (arXiv No. 2210.01790). https://arxiv.org/abs/2210.01790

Silver, D., & Sutton, R. S. (2025, April). Welcome to the era of experience [White paper]. *DeepMind*. https://storage.googleapis.com/deepmind-media/Era-of-Experience/The%20Era%20of%20Experience%20Paper.pdf

Soares, N., & Fallenstein, B. (2017). Agent foundations for aligning machine intelligence with human interests: A technical research agenda. In V. Müller (Ed.), *The technological singularity* (pp. 103–127). Springer.

Sorensen, T., Jiang, L., Hwang, J. D., Levine, S., Pyatkin, V., West, P., Dziri, N., Lu, X., Rao, K., Bhagavatula, C., Sap, M., Tasioulas, J., & Choi, Y. (2024). Value kaleidoscope: Engaging AI with pluralistic human values, rights, and duties. In *Proceedings of the AAAI Conference on Artificial Intelligence, 38*(18), 19937–19947.

Sullivan, M. (2025, May 30). Why I'm getting worried about AI safety. https://www.linkedin.com/pulse/why-im-getting-worried-ai-safety-fast-company-senze/

Tegmark, M. (2025, February 21). *Superintelligent agents pose catastrophic risks: Can Scientist AI offer a safer path?* arXiv. https://arxiv.org/abs/2502.15657

Tomasik, B. (2019, January 3). *Artificial intelligence and its implications for future suffering*. Effective Altruism Forum. https://longtermrisk.org/artificial-intelligence-and-its-implications-for-future-suffering/

UNESCO. (2021). *Recommendation on the ethics of artificial intelligence*. UNESCO Publishing.

Wiener, N. (1960). Some moral and technical consequences of automation. *Science, 131*(3410), 1355–1358.

Yampolskiy, R. V. (2025). *Considerations on the AI endgame: Ethics, risks and computational frameworks*. Routledge.

Yang, J., Tan, R., Wu, Q., Zheng, R., Peng, B., Liang, Y., Gu, Y., Cai, M., Ye, S., Jang, J., Deng, Y., Liden, L., & Gao, J. (2025). *Magma: A foundation model for multimodal AI agents* (arXiv:2502.13130). arXiv.

Yudkowsky, E. (2008). Artificial intelligence as a positive and negative factor in global risk. In N. Bostrom & M. M. Ćirković (Eds.), *Global catastrophic risks* (pp. 308–345). Oxford University Press.

Yudkowsky, E. (2023, March 29). Pausing AI developments isn't enough. We need to shut it all down. *TIME*. https://time.com/6266923/ai-eliezer-yudkowsky-open-letter-not-enough/

Yudkowsky, E. (2025, May 26). Eliezer Yudkowsky: Artificial Intelligence and the End of Humanity https://www.youtube.com/watch?v=0QmDcQIvSDc

Zeng, Y., Huang, W., Jiang, L., … Huang, G. (2025). *S²-MAD: Breaking the token barrier to enhance multi-agent debate efficiency* [Preprint]. arXiv. https://arxiv.org/abs/2502.04790

Zhang, H., Cui, Z., Wang, X., Zhang, Q., Wang, Z., Wu, D., & Hu, S. (2025). *If multi-agent debate is the answer, what is the question?* [Preprint]. arXiv. https://arxiv.org/abs/2502.08788

Ziv, L. (2025, May 18). The top agentic AI security threats you need to know in 2025. *Lasso Security Blog*. https://www.lasso.security/blog/agentic-ai-security-threats-2025

PART III

Applications

CHAPTER 6

Intelligence Diversity and Educational Transformation Through AI Pluralism

Alan H. Coverstone

Abstract This chapter argues that intelligence diversity, rooted in Howard Gardner's theory of multiple intelligences, provides the essential epistemological foundation for AI pluralism and educational transformation. Generative AI systems excel at the narrow linguistic and logical-mathematical tasks that have dominated traditional education. This chapter exposes the inadequacy of intelligence singularity paradigms that marginalize other valid forms of human knowing. Drawing on Dewey's pragmatism, Haraway's situated knowledges, and Hegel's dialectical method, the author demonstrates how recognizing multiple intelligences challenges the singular intelligence model structuring both educational assessment and AI development. The chapter examines how AI systems trained on data reflecting educational biases toward linguistic and logical reasoning perpetuate these narrow conceptions of intelligence. To counter this, the author proposes intelligence diversity as cognitive infrastructure for AI pluralism, arguing that cultivating multiple ways of knowing prepares students for meaningful human-AI collaboration. The chapter advocates for pedagogical approaches like debate that engage diverse

A. H. Coverstone (✉)
Director, Regional Partnerships, National Speech & Debate Association,
Fairfax, VA, USA
e-mail: alan.coverstone@speechanddebate.org

P. A. Rao (ed.), *AI Pluralism*,
https://doi.org/10.1007/978-3-032-06558-2_6

intelligences, moving beyond the fact-versus-opinion binary toward "epistemic contestation"that embraces uncertainty and multiplicity. This transformation positions intelligence diversity not as accommodation for human limitation, but as recognition of cognitive abundance essential for democratic education and ethical AI development.

Keywords Intelligence diversity • multiple intelligences • AI pluralism • educational transformation • Gardner's MI theory • debate pedagogy • cognitive diversity • educational equity • human-AI collaboration • epistemic contestation

A single-intelligence approach will be both insufficient for the complexity of global challenges and precarious in a world where generative AI can outperform humans on standardized tasks.

6.1 Introduction: Reimagining Intelligence in the AI Era

6.1.1 *Preface: Intelligence Diversity as the Epistemological Foundation of AI Pluralism*

What do we mean by "intelligence"? For over a century, formal education systems have treated intelligence as a singular construct—fixed, measurable, and computational—defined by what standardized tests can assess: primarily logical-mathematical and linguistic reasoning. This narrow conception, reinforced by psychometric traditions and institutionalized through curriculum, pedagogy, and policy, has long marginalized other valid forms of human knowing. Yet today, the rise of generative AI systems capable of excelling at precisely those standardized tasks—essay writing, problem-solving, even test-taking—exposes the deep inadequacies of our traditional definitions. If machines now outperform humans at what we've labeled as "intelligent," we are forced to ask: were those ever sufficient measures of human potential in the first place?

This chapter argues that only a commitment to intelligence diversity—understood as a plurality of irreducible ways of knowing—can sustain human agency in an AI-saturated world.

Intelligence diversity does not merely call for better teaching methods or more inclusive classrooms. It calls for a different epistemological architecture—one in which pluralism is not a concession to human limitation but a reflection of the richness of our cognitive ecology.

From this perspective, AI pluralism is not just a technical design philosophy; it is the logical consequence of affirming that intelligence itself is multiple, contextual, and situated. Without intelligence diversity, AI pluralism is incoherent. And without education as the site where diverse intelligences are recognized, developed, and made legible, neither intelligence diversity nor AI pluralism can be sustained.

Gardner's Multiple Intelligences (MI) theory envisions intelligence as the capacity to solve problems and create products valued within specific cultures (Gardner, 1983). Framing intelligences of diverse modalities (spatial, musical, etc.) provides a crucial cognitive framework for acknowledging Haraway's concept of situated knowledge. Different intelligences are inherently different "partial perspectives," rooted in varied embodied experiences, cultural contexts, and ways of engaging with the world (Haraway, 1988). MI offers a cognitive framework aligned with Haraway's socio-cultural notion of situated knowledge. This alignment is critical amid the pursuit of artificial general intelligence (AGI) and artificial superhuman intelligence (ASI), which enacts a new iteration of the "god trick" on a superhuman scale beyond the capacity of human intelligence to critique.

In spaces of education, cultivation of diverse intelligences, particularly through practices like debate pedagogy, can be grounded in Dewey's concept of democracy as collective inquiry (Dewey, 1916, 1938a). Different intelligences contribute diverse *forms* of hypotheses, evidence, and reasoning styles into a Deweyan process of experimental and experiential problem-solving (Dewey, 1910, 1939). The interaction and negotiation between viewpoints grounded in these distinct intelligences reveals a Hegelian tension between perspectives arising from different cognitive modalities. Such tensions can, through structured interaction, lead to a higher-order understanding or *sublation* that transcends individual perspectives while preserving elements of each (Hegel, 1812/1969).

AI pluralism requires technological ecosystems that represent a diversity of values, perspectives, and problem-solving approaches. The epistemic infrastructure for such systems, particularly in supporting meaningful coexistence between human and machine intelligences, must be grounded in the recognition and cultivation of this cognitive diversity described by MI theory.

For much of the twentieth century, educational systems around the world—especially in the United States—have revolved around the notion of intelligence as a single, fixed construct (Gould, 1996). Whether defined by IQ scores, college admissions tests, or accountability exams, "smartness" came to be narrowly measured by performance in logical-mathematical and linguistic tasks, assessing individual recall and syllogistic application of prior established "knowns" that we have named "facts" (Gardner, 1983; Sternberg, 1985). Although such skills are undoubtedly important, the exclusive emphasis on one way of knowing (epistemology) has fostered systemic inequities, hampered the development of students with other cognitive strengths, and shaped entire generations of learners to chase a narrow band of intellectual achievement (Freire, 1970; Anyon, 1980; Reardon, 2011; Darling-Hammond, 2010; Flynn, 2007).

Today's artificial intelligence systems are not encroaching equally on *all* human intelligences, but rather excelling in the specific intelligence modalities that have long been privileged under the assumption of intelligence singularity, especially those associated with linguistic precision, symbolic manipulation, and logical inference (Turing, 1950; Newell & Simon, 1976; Manning et al., 2008). These capacities, often treated as the apex of human intelligence in standardized schooling and psychometric evaluation, have now been operationalized at scale through computational architectures (Gould, 1996; Gardner, 1983). As a result, the fundamental mismatch between education systems rooted in this narrow conception of intelligence and the broader plurality of human cognitive experience is no longer a mere philosophical concern; it is revealing a structural crisis (Haraway, 1988; Sorensen et al., 2024).

Traditional schooling, by continuing to prioritize singular forms of intelligence, and approaches to AI design which explicitly chase intelligence singularity, not only marginalize other ways of knowing, but also train AI systems to replicate and scale the very biases that underlie that marginalization (Eubanks, 2017; Noble, 2018; Selwyn, 2019). In doing so, both institutions—education and AI—collude in a feedback loop that reinforces the hegemony of a single epistemological model, while rendering alternative intelligences increasingly invisible, illegible, or obsolete (Sorensen et al., 2024; Gardner, 1983).

Howard Gardner's theory of multiple intelligences (MI) challenged the single-intelligence paradigm by emphasizing that human intelligence is inherently pluralistic (Gardner, 1983, 1999). Musical, bodily-kinesthetic, interpersonal, intrapersonal, spatial, and naturalistic intelligences are just as integral to human cognition as linguistic or mathematical abilities. Over decades of systemic underemphasis in curricula and assessments, these other intelligences have been devalued, effectively foreclosing educational pathways not only for students whose dominant strengths fall outside linguistic and logical-mathematical domains, but for all learners, each of whom brings a unique and shifting constellation of intelligences to different contexts of learning and performance (Gardner, 1999; Rogoff, 2003). As a result, schools have not only failed to recognize the full spectrum of human capacities but have also left undeveloped many of the skills that remain uniquely human and irreplaceable in an AI-saturated world, including ethical discernment, collaborative problem-solving, and contextual sensitivity (Dewey, 1938b; Freire, 1970).

AI pluralism extends this argument into the realm of machine intelligence. Rather than train AI systems to assume a single version of "rational correctness" or a static notion of "average user," AI pluralism promotes technological ecosystems that represent a diversity of values, perspectives, and problem-solving approaches (Sorensen et al., 2024). When combined with the lens of human intelligence diversity, AI pluralism points toward a future in which human and machine intelligences collaborate across multiple domains, complementing each other's strengths through challenges grounded in contestability and explainability.

Schools have a vital role to play in actualizing this vision. By embracing intelligence diversity as a guiding principle, we can equip students not just with AI literacy, but with the deeper skills necessary to shape AI ethically and responsibly. We can also resist the reductive "fact vs. opinion" binaries that have dominated educational discourse, preparing students to navigate an information environment of uncertain authorship and "fake news." By integrating pluralistic instructional strategies such as debate pedagogy, educators can cultivate multiple intelligences simultaneously, preparing students to engage in a world where AI is ubiquitous yet far from infallible.

This chapter weaves together the history of intelligence singularity in education, Gardner's multiple intelligences framework, the urgent case for reimagining education in an AI-driven era, and debate as a key example of how to operationalize AI pluralism in day-to-day instruction. The underlying message is clear: The era of generative AI demands new forms of educational practice. Intelligence diversity, extended into AI pluralism, can anchor these transformations, ensuring that learners develop the collaborative, ethical, and creative capacities necessary for a safer, more equitable future.

Forty Problems; Forty Minutes
In a middle school math classroom, desks are arranged in silent rows. The students, preparing for an upcoming benchmark exam, work through forty linear equations in forty minutes. The teacher reminds them: "Show your work, no talking."

A student with strong spatial intuition sketches an abstract visual pattern to model the problem but is told to erase it. Another, who thrives in verbal dialogue, silently taps a pencil, waiting for a collaborative moment that never comes.

In this room, speed and syntax define intelligence. Everything else—pattern, movement, conversation, feeling—is irrelevant. The narrowness of the task becomes the narrowness of who is seen as capable.

6.2 The Structural Dominance of Intelligence Singularity in Education

Modern American conceptions of intelligence in public education are deeply rooted in early twentieth-century psychometrics. Alfred Binet and Théodore Simon initially designed the first intelligence test to identify students needing academic support. But in the United States, adaptations like Lewis Terman's Stanford-Binet scale redefined IQ as a measure of hereditary cognitive ability (Kevles, 1998). Terman's work, entangled with eugenic ideologies, used test scores to support social hierarchies and the idea of fixed intellectual capacity. This framing privileged linguistic and logical-mathematical reasoning, cementing their dominance in institutional definitions of intelligence (Gould, 1996).

Building on IQ's authority, standardized admissions tests like the SAT—originating from the Army Alpha Test—and later the ACT, further solidified the belief that intellectual potential could be quantified through time-limited exams (Lemann, 1999). Brigham, an early SAT architect, claimed these tests measured innate academic aptitude, but they soon became stand-ins for intelligence itself. Focused on decontextualized problem-solving in math and reading, these assessments reinforced a narrow cognitive ideal that dictated access to higher education and economic mobility (Lemann, 1999).

Federal policy in the late twentieth and early twenty-first centuries further entrenched this singular view of intelligence. The No Child Left Behind Act (NCLB) of 2001 mandated annual standardized testing in reading and math, linking test scores to school funding (U.S. Congress, 2002; Dee & Jacob, 2011). This high-stakes climate led many schools to narrow their curricula, cutting time for the arts, physical education, speech and debate—disciplines that nurture multiple intelligences (Beveridge, 2009). As a result, bodily-kinesthetic, musical, spatial, interpersonal, and intrapersonal intelligences were increasingly sidelined in favor of those that could be measured on a test (Darling-Hammond, 2007).

As the instructional focus sharpened around test-based performance, students whose strengths lay outside dominant cognitive modes were left with fewer chances to succeed. Under-resourced schools, under pressure to meet Adequate Yearly Progress metrics, often adopted "drill-and-kill" approaches, displacing creative and relational learning (Au, 2007). For students of color, students with special needs, English language learners, and those experiencing poverty, this model frequently functioned as a mechanism of exclusion rather than empowerment (Lipman, 2004; Darling-Hammond, 2007).

Standardized tests also embed cultural and socioeconomic biases. Performance correlates strongly with access to test preparation, familiarity with the testing format, and alignment with dominant language and reasoning styles (Au, 2015). Students whose cultural or cognitive orientations diverge from these norms are often labeled "underperforming"—not for lacking intelligence, but because their intelligences fall outside the narrow frame these tests recognize (Rose, 2016). This misalignment deepens inequities by limiting recognition and opportunity to those who fit a pre-approved cognitive mold.

The legacy of intelligence singularity remains embedded in school practices. AP exams, gifted program placements, and teaching aligned to state benchmarks continue to prioritize performance in linguistic and logical-mathematical tasks (Ladson-Billings, 2014). These remain the dominant currencies of educational success.

Decades of privileging these intelligences have not only limited opportunities for students whose strengths lie elsewhere but have also constrained all learners. Every student enters school with a unique constellation of intelligences—some more developed, others emerging—shaped by culture, experience, and context. Yet classrooms rarely tap into this full range, reducing intelligence to what can be scored, timed, and ranked (Darling-Hammond, 2010; Duckworth et al., 2012).

6.3 Gardner's Theory of Multiple Intelligences: A Broadening Lens

Howard Gardner's theory of multiple intelligences (MI) is often misunderstood as merely a teaching strategy—a tool for differentiated instruction or inclusive curriculum design. But its significance lies deeper: MI redefines what it means to know. It challenges the long-standing assumption that valid knowledge stems from a single, universal mode of reasoning rooted in language, logic, and propositional truth (Gardner, 1983). In doing so, it aligns with the epistemological pluralism proposed in Chap. 1.

John Dewey's pragmatism views democracy as a method for problem-solving through collective inquiry, where diverse perspectives test ideas against lived experience (Dewey, 1938b).

Gardner's framework gives cognitive substance to this process: each intelligence offers a distinct way of posing questions, interpreting data, and making sense of the world. Educational practices like debate pedagogy embody this collective inquiry, nurturing the communication and shared reflection Dewey considered essential to democratic knowledge-building (Hoerr, 2000).

Haraway's concept of situated knowledges complements this perspective by insisting that all perspectives are partial, embodied, and culturally embedded (Haraway, 1988). MI's definition of intelligence as problem-solving valued within specific cultural contexts and its catalog of intelligences including musical, spatial, bodily-kinesthetic, and more maps directly onto this notion. Each intelligence represents a different partial perspective, shaped by neural architecture, cultural practice, and personal experience (Gardner, 1999).

The interaction between these diverse intelligences, especially in settings like debates, can be illuminated by Hegel's dialectical method. For Hegel, contradictions drive intellectual development, producing a higher-order synthesis that transcends initial oppositions (Hegel, 1807/1977). When perspectives grounded in different intelligences—such as a logical analysis and an intuitive spatial insight—interact through structured processes, they can yield new understandings neither perspective could have generated alone. This dialectical understanding reflects the kind of integrative learning MI theory supports.

MI theory thus resists the traditional privileging of abstraction, symbolic logic, and linearity in education. It asserts that humans *also* know through rhythm, movement, emotional resonance, ecological perception, interpersonal interaction, and reflective insight (Gardner, 1999). These are not auxiliary skills or "learning styles," but full-fledged modes of cognition, each with its own logic, truth conditions, and evidentiary standards. Carrying this forward, MI problematizes not just curricular content but the underlying architecture of educational epistemology. In place of the structures of intelligence singularity we conceive here of a pluralistic ontology of mind: no single intelligence is normative, and no learner can be captured by a universal metric situated in only one intelligence.

This reconceptualization has profound implications both for pedagogy and assessment and for how we build and evaluate artificial intelligence. If knowledge itself is plural, then systems that prioritize one mode of reasoning will necessarily fail to represent or interact with the full range of human understanding (Sousa, 2016). MI calls for a fundamental rethinking of epistemic legitimacy. In this light, it also becomes the ontological foundation of AI pluralism: a vision of artificial systems designed not to replicate a single model of thinking, but to engage with and support the full spectrum of human intelligences. MI is not an instructional add-on—it is the epistemic infrastructure for human-machine coexistence.

In *Frames of Mind* (1983), Gardner rejected the unitary concept of intelligence that dominates educational psychology. In its place, he identified distinct intelligences: linguistic, logical-mathematical, musical, bodily-kinesthetic, spatial, interpersonal, and intrapersonal, later adding naturalistic and tentatively proposing existential intelligence (Gardner, 1999). Each represents a unique way of processing information and solving problems.

Gardner's definition of intelligence—the capacity to solve problems or create products valued in particular cultural settings—further disrupts the idea of intelligence as fixed or universal (Gardner, 1983). In different environments, different intelligences are essential. In a coastal fishing village, naturalistic and bodily-kinesthetic intelligences might be paramount; in a technology-driven urban context, linguistic and logical skills might dominate. Intelligence is always culturally situated and plural in function.

MI theory has, of course, faced critique. Psychometricians have questioned whether the intelligences are separable, measurable, or distinct from personality traits (Visser et al., 2006; Waterhouse, 2006). Gardner has responded that MI is not a ranking tool but a framework for recognizing cognitive diversity (Gardner, 2006). Even skeptics often concede that MI challenges the orthodoxy of educational assessment and opens space for more inclusive, creative instruction.

Nonetheless, its integration into American education has been limited. While many teachers incorporate MI-informed methods—such as multimodal lessons or learning stations—these efforts often remain superficial, detached from MI's deeper epistemological challenge (Hoerr, 2000). Standardized testing, narrow achievement metrics, and rigid curricular structures continue to elevate linguistic and logical intelligences, marginalizing others. As a result, MI is often treated as a supplementary idea rather than a transformation of educational paradigms.

Yet, support for MI continues to grow through neuroscience and classroom research.

Neuroimaging shows that different tasks engage distinct brain regions, supporting the theory's claim of modular intelligences. Classroom studies reveal that MI-based instruction can enhance motivation, engagement, and metacognition (Kornhaber et al., 2004). When students can demonstrate learning through performance, construction, or creative expression, they often understand and retain concepts more deeply than when limited to conventional testing.

MI, then, is not merely about better teaching. It offers a radical reimagining of cognition, culture, and learning—a vision crucial to any future where human and artificial intelligences must collaborate, align, and evolve together.

6.4 AI's Reinforcement of Intelligence Singularity

6.4.1 *Schooling the Machine: Education's Role in Shaping Narrow AI*

Modern AI systems, especially large language models (LLMs), are trained on vast body of human-generated data and refined through reinforcement learning with human feedback (RLHF). Though appearing purely technical, this process mirrors the logic of high-stakes standardized education: it prioritizes conformity, penalizes deviation, and rewards correctness within a narrowly defined epistemic frame (Bender & Koller, 2020).

This resemblance is not accidental. Traditional schooling, premised on intelligence singularity, emphasizes memorization, standardized outputs, and procedural correctness. The training of AI models in this same cognitive mold reinforces the dominance of those forms of reasoning while marginalizing others, such as spatial, bodily-kinesthetic, interpersonal, intrapersonal, musical, and naturalistic intelligences.

By reducing its complex training data into an averaged, statistically-optimized voice, AI reproduces and amplifies the same narrow assumptions that structure formal education. This stands in direct opposition to philosophical insights that advocate for epistemic plurality.

Dewey's pragmatism insists that knowledge arises through collective, experiential inquiry (Dewey, 1938a). Haraway's "situated knowledges" critique the notion of an objective, disembodied perspective and expose the biases masked by such a view (Haraway, 1988). Hegel's dialectical method proposes that intellectual progress depends on engaging and transforming contradictions rather than erasing them (Hegel, 1807/1977).

In privileging uniform correctness, dominant AI development undermines the very contradictions and partial perspectives that catalyze new knowledge. In suppressing dissent to generate synthetic averages, AI enacts Haraway's "god trick"—a falsely universal view that hides the partiality of its data. In doing so, AI and traditional education form a feedback loop that reinforces a single epistemological paradigm, further obscuring alternative intelligences and ways of knowing.

6.4.2 *The Collapse of Cognitive Interdependence*

Historically, humans built knowledge collectively. Modernization was built on the assumption that no individual could access or process all information needed to thrive in community alone, which necessitated a reliance on cognitive interdependence: the integration of partial insights from different people, fields, and modalities. This pragmatic pluralism was not originally grounded in a philosophical commitment to diversity but rather in a functional need to compensate for individual cognitive limitations.

AI has profoundly altered this dynamic. Within the dominant computational-linguistic paradigm that also shapes formal education, AI systems simulate omniscience—processing vast data at superhuman speed and delivering optimized outputs that appear comprehensive. This creates the illusion of epistemic mastery, which displaces the need for distributed human cognition and collaboration.

But this shift exposes the weakness of pluralism built on necessity alone. Because it never rested on a principled belief in cognitive diversity, pragmatic pluralism becomes dispensable once AI appears to eliminate the limits it addressed. The result is a subtle epistemic shift: human variance from AI outputs is no longer seen as a complementary perspective, but as error or inefficiency. In this context, the social scaffolding that supported pluralism begins to erode.

This trend, already well underway in America, is especially dangerous because it ignores the deeper pluralism articulated in Gardner's theory of multiple intelligences (1999), which argues that human beings engage the world through fundamentally different modalities of knowing— not as tools or styles, but as irreducible cognitive systems. An artificial intelligence that erases intelligence diversity will do the same to people with strengths in diverse intelligences and to those parts of our humanity that distinguish us from the machines.

6.4.3 Rebuilding on Principle: A Pluralism of Diversity

To resist this collapse, pluralism must be re-founded on an ontological claim: that human intelligence is inherently plural, not because of our limitations, but because of our diversity. This requires a shift from a pluralism of necessity to a pluralism of abundance.

Gardner's MI theory provides the conceptual infrastructure for this transition. By identifying linguistic, logical-mathematical, spatial, bodily-kinesthetic, musical, interpersonal, intrapersonal, and naturalistic intelligences, MI challenges the idea of a singular cognitive norm and asserts that knowing itself is diverse (Gardner, 1999). Knowledge is not a unitary process but one that unfolds differently depending on the knower, the task, and the cultural context.

This position aligns with key philosophical foundations: Haraway's situated knowledges emphasize that all cognition is partial and embodied; Dewey's pragmatism sees knowledge as emerging from collaborative problem-solving; Hegel's dialectics require a clash of distinct perspectives to drive transformation. MI embodies the philosophical foundations of pluralism by asserting that diverse intelligences provide the necessary viewpoints for inquiry (Dewey, 1916, 1938), embodiment for epistemic legitimacy (Haraway, 1988), and contradiction for dialectical synthesis (Hegel, 1812/1969).

Pluralism, then, must be embraced not just as a strategy for inclusion but as a framework for truth itself—one that acknowledges that knowledge does not emerge from singular, computational optimization, but from the interaction and contestation of multiple, irreducible ways of knowing.

The path forward requires a reconceptualization of pluralism. It must be rebuilt not on what humans lack, but on what humans are. Pluralism must no longer be a concession to limitation; it must become a design principle grounded in the diversity of intelligences through which human beings make meaning (Gardner, 1999; Haraway, 1988). This is not a return to the old pluralism—it is a movement toward something more durable, more just, and more aligned with our epistemic ecology.

6.4.4 *Toward AI Pluralism by Design*

To remain aligned with human cognition, future AI systems should be reoriented around epistemic pluralism, not singular optimization. AI should be evaluated not just on its ability to produce correct answers, but on its capacity to reflect diverse reasoning styles, cultural understandings, and value systems.

This work is already underway in emerging approaches to AI pluralism. Steerable pluralism models such as Constitutional AI, allow users to prompt perspective-specific outputs based on values, drawing on advances in aligning large language models to ethical or ideological frameworks through prompt engineering and reinforcement mechanisms (Bai et al., 2022). Distributional pluralism calibrates outputs to reflect a community's internal diversity, rather than defaulting to a misleading consensus or median viewpoint. Overton pluralism aims to present a full spectrum of reasonable viewpoints, mirroring the Overton Window framework in public discourse, which defines the range of politically acceptable ideas within a society. Each of these methods operationalizes the philosophical and cognitive insights that underlie Multiple Intelligences (MI) theory, recognizing that intelligence is culturally situated and functionally diverse (Gardner, 1983; Haraway, 1988).

These developments are more than mere technical adjustments. They represent a new epistemological order, one that demands AI systems be designed to interpret and engage with the full span of human intelligences. AI pluralism becomes a necessary corrective to the legacy of intelligence singularity. It ensures that artificial systems do not just replicate a narrow form of cognition, but participate in—and enhance—the complex, pluralistic ecology of human knowing.

This principled epistemological stance insists that truth emerges not from computational maximums, but from the interaction, overlap, and contestation of multiple, irreducible ways of knowing.

6.5 Intelligence Diversity as Epistemological Infrastructure

We need a fundamentally different conception of pluralism, a "pluralism of diversity," rooted in the ontological claim that human intelligence is itself a cognitively and culturally plural system.

Howard Gardner's theory of multiple intelligences (MI) offers the essential epistemological infrastructure required for this reconstruction. Gardner's framework provides a way of rethinking what intelligence is, how it functions, and why no single modality can claim total epistemic authority.

In contrast to the singular intelligence paradigm where intelligence is viewed as a fixed, general capacity measured primarily through logical-mathematical and linguistic proficiency, Gardner posits that human intelligence is multiple, dynamic, and contextually expressed.

Linguistic, logical-mathematical, spatial, bodily-kinesthetic, musical, interpersonal, intrapersonal, naturalistic, and potentially existential intelligences represent irreducible ways of knowing, not auxiliary learning styles or mere talents.

This reconceptualization changes everything. It means that knowledge itself is not singular. There is no universal mode through which all truths are accessed or all problems solved. Instead, knowing is itself a plural phenomenon. It unfolds through different cognitive channels depending on the knower, the context, the community, and the task.

From this view, pluralism is not a concession to ignorance or limitation, it is an ontological imperative. It reflects the actual structure of human cognition and the ecology of thought that makes collective knowledge possible. If we accept this premise, then pluralism is not merely a cultural ideal but a necessary epistemic condition for any system—educational, political, or technological—that seeks alignment with human cognition.

Intelligence diversity provides the foundation upon which AI pluralism must rest. AI pluralism becomes viable only when intelligence diversity is taken as foundational. Designing AI pluralistic systems means building architectures that can interpret, support, and interact with multiple human intelligences in ways that embody the philosophical principles of inquiry, situated knowledge, and sublation.

Haraway (1988) insists that all knowledge is partial and embodied, emerging from specific positions. Recognizing multiple intelligences validates ways of knowing, such as spatial or musical understanding, that fall outside the dominant linguistic-logical paradigm. AI architectures that can interpret and support these diverse modalities directly respond to Haraway's call to surface and sustain epistemically marginalized perspectives historically devalued by systems focused on intelligence as singularity. By valuing these different modes of knowing, AI supports a more accountable epistemology that recognizes the partial, situated nature of all knowledge.

Enabling interaction with multiple human intelligences similarly advances Dewey's (1916, 1938b) emphasis on collective inquiry and problem-solving. For Dewey, truth emerges not from abstract knowledge but from the dynamic testing and revision of ideas through communication, negotiation, and shared reflection among diverse individuals. AI systems designed to interact with humans expressing ideas through different MI modalities—whether through linguistic debate, analyzing spatial designs, responding to emotional cues (interpersonal/intrapersonal), or evaluating physical actions (bodily-kinesthetic)— facilitate this iterative, social process of knowledge creation. This interactive capacity operationalizes Dewey's vision of democracy as an epistemic process.

Interpreting reasoning across different intelligence modalities also facilitates the kind of dialectical exchange central to Hegelian sublation. Hegel (1807/1977) argued that contradictions are essential to generating new knowledge through sublation, the simultaneous preservation, negation, and transcendence of opposing viewpoints. For pluralistic systems to metabolize contradictions into emergent forms of knowledge, they must be able to understand and hold tension between different perspectives. AI can help identify the complementarities and tensions between these views, contributing to the Hegelian process where insights from different modalities are not erased but elevated into a higher-order understanding.

Education is the crucial infrastructure through which this epistemic vision must be enacted. It is where students will learn not only how to use AI, but how to remain epistemically plural in the face of machine singularity. It is where the full spectrum of intelligences must be cultivated so that learners are prepared not just to operate alongside AI, but to shape and constrain it in service of more inclusive, participatory forms of knowledge.

In this model, intelligence diversity is not an accommodation—it is the architecture of future knowledge systems. It is what makes human co-intelligence with AI both possible and ethical. Without it, AI pluralism collapses into a simulacrum of diversity. With it, pluralism becomes the epistemic logic of a truly human-centered future.

6.6 The Collapse of Fact vs. Opinion: Reframing Knowledge Through Intelligence Diversity

Building on the epistemological framework laid out in the previous sections, we now turn to a real-world site where pluralism grounded in intelligence diversity can clarify and enrich our understanding of contested knowledge. The collapse of the simplistic **fact vs. opinion** binary, especially in AI-mediated information environments reveals how urgently we need pedagogical approaches that equip students to navigate uncertainty, multiplicity, and epistemic complexity. This section shows how intelligence diversity reframes our understanding of factuality, credibility, and interpretation in the age of AI.

6.6.1 Fact vs. Opinion as an Oversimplification

In Western education, the distinction between "fact" (objective, verifiable truth) and "opinion" (subjective, personal belief) has long structured classroom discourse. Students are routinely taught to label statements accordingly, with "facts" associated with definitive answers in math and science grounded in "known" data and repeatable computations, while "opinions" appear in essays or moral debates conceptualized as *deficient* in data and computation. This fuzzy binary underwrites not only test questions but entire pedagogical approaches.

MI complicates this dichotomy: no fact emerges from a single cognitive act. The formation of scientific knowledge requires logical-mathematical modeling, spatial visualization, interpersonal peer review, and often intrapersonal judgment about interpretation and application (Gardner, 1999). In short, "facts" themselves are not products of a single intelligence—they are cognitively plural artifacts (Kitcher, 2011).

Take the example of climate change. The claim "climate change is occurring" appears as a scientific fact grounded in overwhelming empirical evidence. But its credibility depends on data modeling (logical-mathematical), pattern recognition (naturalistic), visual system design (spatial), and institutional consensus (interpersonal). Presenting this as a purely "objective" statement flattens the complex pluralism of intelligences that supports it and counterintuitively weakens its persuasive utility when assessed from different frames of intelligence (Gardner, 2006).

Plural cognition explains disagreement not as fact denial, but differing intelligence engagement. Understanding this does not mean relativizing all claims into mere opinion, but rather broadening our sense of how truth is constructed, and why some people may resist or misunderstand a claim depending on how it's framed, delivered, or aligned with and interpreted through their dominant intelligences (Kitcher, 2011).

Rather than collapse into nihilism, this recognition opens the door to a more empathetic, dialogic understanding of contested claims. It replaces binary opposition with epistemic humility and *invites pluralistic negotiation* over what counts as valid and persuasive—especially across different communities, cultures, and cognitive modes.

6.6.2 Permanent Uncertainty of Authorship

Artificial intelligence introduces a new layer of complexity. Generative tools such as large language models can now produce vast volumes of text that closely imitate human authorship.

As these systems become increasingly integrated into writing, content production, and even journalism, we are entering an age of permanent uncertainty of authorship.

Traditional epistemic validation relied heavily on knowing who authored a claim—whether through institutional affiliation, disciplinary standing, or a reputation for expertise. But with AI- generated content, authorship becomes opaque, distributed, or even absent. Students, educators, and citizens alike can no longer assume that a well-formed sentence has a traceable human origin. This erosion of authorship undermines conventional fact-checking, which often depended on verifying source credibility as a proxy for truth.

What we face now is not just uncertainty about what is true, but who is even speaking or asserting truth, and whether the speaker is even attempting to reason and understand. Uncertainty of authorship raises significant questions about the nature of personal responsibility and whether it can even be ascertained at all.

6.6.3 *Unverifiable AI Reasoning*

Compounding this issue is the fact that AI's "reasoning" is not transparent. While a scientist can often explain the chain of logic behind a conclusion, an AI's response emerges from a probabilistic model trained on massive corpora. Its logic is statistical, not discursive; inferential, but not accountable.

Even developers struggle to explain why a particular output was generated. The AI does not truly "know" in any human sense, nor can it self-reflect, revise, or justify its conclusions. As a result, it can produce statements that *sound* factual but lack grounding in any verifiable or interpretable reasoning process. The appearance of intelligent conclusions masks a fundamental absence of understanding the arguments in the first place.

In this context, the distinction between fact and opinion becomes even more unstable. AI can generate both with equal fluency, often indistinguishably. This calls for a new kind of literacy, not just in what to believe or know, but in how claims are constructed, reasoned, and situated within broader epistemic contexts.

6.6.4 *Educational Implications: Teaching "Epistemic Contestation"*

As AI collapses the clarity of authorship and the integrity of reasoning, schools must adopt new pedagogical strategies. We can no longer afford to teach students to simply identify "the right answer" or to memorize disciplinary facts. Instead, we must cultivate the skill of epistemic contestation: the ability to navigate competing truth claims, evaluate partial evidence, and engage in argumentation that embraces and fosters sense-making in the face of perpetual uncertainty.

Intelligence diversity becomes a pedagogical imperative. Different intelligences offer different tools for epistemic evaluation, for example:

- Logical-mathematical intelligence supports data analysis and inference.
- Interpersonal intelligence fosters critical dialogue and collaborative sense-making.
- Intrapersonal intelligence aids in ethical reflection and intellectual self-awareness.
- Spatial and bodily-kinesthetic intelligences contribute experiential insight and embodied reasoning.

Students must be taught not just to ask "*Is this claim true?*" but "*How is this claim supported?*" and "*Which intelligences are being activated or neglected in this interpretation?*" This transforms the act of learning from absorbing static truths into engaging dynamic, pluralistic processes of inquiry.

Understanding the work of disciplinary experts remains important, but the goal should not be passive acceptance of expert conclusions. Rather, students should learn to analyze the intelligences and epistemic practices behind those conclusions, testing how they align or diverge from other ways of knowing.

Through this approach, we move beyond the fact/opinion binary and into a model of knowledge as constructed, contested, and plural—a domain where human and artificial intelligences must be critically engaged, not blindly trusted. This is the foundation for epistemic pluralism in a post- singularity world: not certainty, but responsibility.

6.7 Intelligence Diversity and the Design of Equitable, AI-Integrated Education

6.7.1 From Epistemic Urgency to Educational Transformation

The dominance of a singular intelligence model—centered on linguistic and logical- mathematical reasoning—has long privileged specific cultural norms and cognitive styles. Standardized tests, IQ assessments, and curricula that elevate abstract, symbolic reasoning embed structural inequities across education, employment, and public discourse (Au, 2007). Those whose strengths align with this narrow model are more likely to succeed in school, gain access to elite institutions, and rise to positions of influence, consolidating epistemic authority and excluding other valid ways of knowing (Gardner, 1999).

This narrowing becomes self-perpetuating. Educational systems often train students to reproduce accepted conclusions rather than construct understanding through diverse cognitive pathways.

When these sanctioned views are challenged—by marginalized groups, dissenters, or cultural outsiders—responses often fail, lacking the pluralistic tools to address disagreement or rebuild trust. The resulting erosion of confidence in expertise is not only political but epistemological, rooted in the failure of intelligence singularity.

Rebuilding shared understanding requires rejecting truth as the exclusive domain of a cognitive elite. Legitimacy must be co-constructed through diverse intelligences engaged in pluralistic reasoning (Gardner, 2016). Intelligence diversity is not just pedagogically sound—it is morally essential. Without it, we deepen alienation, escalate polarization, and lose the ability to collaboratively address crises that demand shared understanding and epistemic empathy (Dewey, 1938a, 1938b).

This urgency intensifies in an AI-integrated future. As artificial systems automate tasks involving linguistic precision and procedural logic, the remaining vital human roles will center on creativity, ethics, emotional intelligence, and collaboration—capacities shaped by often marginalized intelligences. Cultivating these intelligences is not peripheral but central to education's purpose (Gardner & Davis, 2013).

6.7.2 Curriculum and Assessment for Pluralistic Intelligence

Realizing this epistemic shift requires embedding cognitive diversity into the core of curriculum and assessment—not merely celebrating it rhetorically (Tomlinson & McTighe, 2006).

Kinesthetic, musical, interpersonal, and other less-privileged intelligences must be integrated into core academic work, not confined to extracurricular edges (Gardner, 1999).

Curricula should include performance-based tasks that engage a range of intelligences. Bodily- kinesthetic learners might build understanding through design challenges or role-play; spatial and musical intelligences through architectural visualization or multimedia composition; interpersonal and intrapersonal intelligences through collaborative work and reflective writing (Darling-Hammond et al., 2019).

For example, a culminating unit on environmental justice might combine ecological observation (naturalistic), community interviews (interpersonal), land use mapping (spatial), data interpretation (logical-mathematical), and public advocacy through speech, performance, or visual art (linguistic, musical, bodily-kinesthetic) (Gardner, 2011). Intelligence, in this model, is not an abstract trait but a capacity enacted in purposeful, context-sensitive ways.

Assessments must evolve accordingly. Rather than rewarding speed, recall, and conformity, rubrics should elevate creativity, ethical judgment, adaptive reasoning, and collaborative inquiry—the real indicators of pluralistic intelligence in action. Teachers must be trained to recognize and support this diversity of excellence.

6.7.3 *Teacher Preparation and Human-AI Co-Intelligence*

To implement a pluralistic curriculum, we need educators prepared to teach pluralistically. Teachers must know how to design instruction that activates multiple intelligences, assess diverse understandings, and navigate the epistemic and ethical complexities of working with AI (Darling-Hammond et al., 2017). They must also reflect critically on their own cognitive preferences and cultural positions, becoming curators of epistemic diversity in the classroom (Ladson-Billings, 2014).

Educators must neither reject AI outright nor defer to it blindly. Instead, they should collaborate with AI tools while maintaining a human-centered focus on cognition, dialogue, and care. In doing so, they model and teach the very capacities students will need in an AI-saturated world: intellectual humility, multimodal literacy, and the ability to engage across cognitive, cultural, and technological boundaries.

6.7.4 *Debate Pedagogy as a Crucible for Intelligence Diversity*

Debate pedagogy models pluralism—not merely as a contest, but also as collaborative inquiry grounded in humility and cognitive diversity (Snider & Schnurer, 2006). Properly structured, debate enacts pluralism. It shifts the focus from winning arguments to constructing and contesting knowledge through varied intelligences (Davis et al., 2016).

Debates, unlike tests, demand multimodal reasoning and ethical engagement along with linguistic fluency, logical structure, interpersonal awareness, self-reflection, and in some formats, spatial, kinesthetic, or musical expression through movement, visuals, or storytelling (Fine, 2001).

In an era when AI can generate coherent claims but lacks accountability, debate highlights the human skill of navigating disagreement. Students must examine claims from multiple angles, anticipate rebuttals, revise stances, and engage ethically with contrasting views. They learn "intelligence translation"—the ability to communicate reasoning across epistemologies and cognitive styles—essential for dialogue in pluralistic systems.

Debate also challenges the flattened epistemologies of both standardized testing and most AI systems. It shows that truth is not an answer to be recalled, but a process of shared inquiry, dynamic synthesis, and creative reasoning. As such, debate functions as both pedagogical tool and civic rehearsal: preparing students not only for academic success, but for ethical citizenship and epistemic collaboration in a diverse, AI-integrated society.

6.8 Epilogue: Reclaiming the Future Through Intelligence Diversity

As generative AI redefines the boundaries of what machines can do, the most urgent challenge for human society is not simply to adapt, but to reimagine the architecture of knowing itself.

Intelligence, long treated as a singular capacity measured through narrow proxies of logic and language, has now met its computational match. But rather than heralding the obsolescence of human cognition, this moment invites us to reclaim the full spectrum of our cognitive potential.

The concept of intelligence diversity—anchored in Gardner's theory of multiple intelligences and extended through emerging theories of digital and distributed cognition—offers a foundation for this reclamation. It insists that no single form of problem-solving, expression, or understanding can exhaust the range of what it means to be intelligent. It reminds us that musical reasoning, spatial imagination, interpersonal intuition, and moral discernment are not merely educational supplements, but vital components of a pluralistic epistemology.

Educational systems that cling to singularity in the name of rigor or efficiency not only fail to prepare students for a world infused with AI, they collude in the production of obsolescence, rendering both students and teachers less capable of engaging with a rapidly changing reality. The epistemic crisis is already underway: when machines outperform humans at the very tasks we've used to define intelligence, we are forced to ask what remains uniquely human. The answer lies not in retreat, but in expansion of what we teach, how we teach, and whom we recognize as capable of deep, valuable knowing.

AI pluralism represents more than a technical alternative to model design; it is the ethical and pedagogical imperative of our time. It calls for systems that are not only interoperable across tasks, but accountable to the heterogeneity of human thought. Just as ecological biodiversity ensures the resilience of natural systems, cognitive and cultural pluralism are the conditions for sustainable educational and technological futures.

In this vision, schools are not pipelines for cognitive conformity, but Empowerment Enclaves; spaces where the cultivation of distinct intelligences becomes the ground for collective action. In these future classrooms, educators do not transmit knowledge from a fixed canon, but orchestrate Collaborative Learning Scenarios in which students discover, apply, and refine diverse modes of inquiry. AI systems, reimagined through the lens of pluralism, become collaborators in these scenarios, scaffolding rather than replacing human meaning-making.

The task before us is therefore not to compete with machines, but to rediscover what it means to be human amidst them. Intelligence diversity, operationalized through AI pluralism, offers both the critique and the construction we need. It exposes the limitations of inherited paradigms while charting a path toward new forms of flourishing: intellectual, ethical, and civic.

To follow that path requires courage, creativity, and a radical commitment to the multiplicity of minds.

References

Anyon, J. (1980). Social class and the hidden curriculum of work. *Journal of Education, 162*(1), 67–92.

Au, W. (2007). High-stakes testing and curricular control: A qualitative metasynthesis. *Educational Researcher, 36*(5), 258–267. https://doi.org/10.3102/0013189X07306523

Au, W. (2015). Meritocracy 2.0: High-stakes, standardized testing as a racial project of neoliberal multiculturalism. *Educational Policy, 30*(1), 39–62. https://doi.org/10.1177/0895904815614916

Bai, Y., Kadavath, S., Kundu, S., Askell, A., Kernion, J., Jones, A., Chen, A., Goldie, A., Mirhoseini, A., McKinnon, C., Chen, C., Olsson, C., Olah, C., Hernandez, D., Drain, D., Ganguli, D., Li, D., Tran-Johnson, E., Perez, E., Kerr, J., Mueller, J., Ladish, J., Landau, J., Ndousse, K., Lukosuite, K., Lovitt, L., Sellitto, M., Elhage, N., Schiefer, N., Mercado, N., DasSarma, N., Lasenby, R., Larson, R., Ringer, S., Johnston, S., Kravec, S., El Showk, S., Fort, S., Lanham, T., Telleen-Lawton, T., Conerly, T., Henigan, T., Hume, T., Bowman, S., Hatfield-Dodds, Z., Mann, B., Amodei, D., Joseph, N., McCandish, S., Brown, T., Kaplan, J. (2022). *Constitutional AI: Harmlessness from AI feedback*. arXiv preprint. https://doi.org/10.48550/arXiv.2212.08073

Bender, E. M., & Koller, A. (2020). Climbing towards NLU: On meaning, form, and understanding in the age of data. In *Proceedings of the 58th Annual Meeting of the Association for Computational Linguistics*, 5185–5198. https://doi.org/10.18653/v1/2020.acl-main.463

Beveridge, T. (2009). No Child Left Behind and fine arts classes. *Arts Education Policy Review, 111*(1), 4–7. https://doi.org/10.1080/10632910903228090

Darling-Hammond, L. (2007). Race, inequality and educational accountability: The irony of "No Child Left Behind". *Race Ethnicity and Education, 10*(3), 245–260. https://doi.org/10.1080/13613320701503207

Darling-Hammond, L. (2010). *The flat world and education: How America's commitment to equity will determine our future*. Teachers College Press.

Darling-Hammond, L., Flook, L., Cook-Harvey, C., Barron, B., & Osher, D. (2019). Implications for educational practice of the science of learning and development. *Applied Developmental Science, 24*(2), 97–140.

Darling-Hammond, L., Hyler, M. E., & Gardner, M. (2017). *Effective teacher professional development*. Learning Policy Institute.

Davis, K. A., Wade Zorwick, M. L., Roland, J., & Maxcy Wade, M. M. (2016). *Using debate in the classroom: Encouraging critical thinking, communication, and collaboration*. Routledge.

Dee, T. S., & Jacob, B. (2011). The impact of No Child Left Behind on student achievement. *Journal of Policy Analysis and Management, 30*(3), 418–446. https://doi.org/10.1002/pam.20586

Dewey, J. (1910). *How we think*. D.C. Heath & Co.

Dewey, J. (1916). *Democracy and education: An introduction to the philosophy of education*. Palgrave Macmillan.

Dewey, J. (1938a). *Logic: The theory of inquiry*. Henry Holt.

Dewey, J. (1938b). *Experience and education*. Palgrave Macmillan.

Dewey, J. (1939). *Creative democracy—The task before us*.

Duckworth, A. L., Quinn, P. D., & Tsukayama, E. (2012). What No Child Left Behind leaves behind: The roles of IQ and self-control in predicting standardized achievement test scores and report card grades. *Journal of Educational Psychology, 104*(2), 439–451. https://doi.org/10.1037/a0026280

Eubanks, V. (2017). *Automating inequality: How high-tech tools profile, police, and punish the poor*. St. Martin's Press.

Fine, G. A. (2001). *Gifted tongues: High school debate and adolescent culture*. Princeton University Press.

Flynn, J. R. (2007). *What is intelligence?: Beyond the Flynn effect*. Cambridge University Press.

Freire, P. (1970). *Pedagogy of the oppressed*. Herder and Herder.

Gardner, H. (1983). *Frames of mind: The theory of multiple intelligences*. Basic Books.

Gardner, H. (1999). *Intelligence reframed: Multiple intelligences for the 21st century*. Basic Books.

Gardner, H. (2006). *Multiple intelligences: New horizons* (Rev. ed.). Basic Books/ Hachette Book Group.

Gardner, H. (2011). *Frames of mind: The theory of multiple intelligences* (3rd ed.). Basic Books.

Gardner, H., & Davis, K. (2013). *The app generation: How today's youth navigate identity, intimacy, and imagination in a digital world*. Yale University Press.

Gould, S. J. (1996). *The mismeasure of man* (Rev. ed.). W. W. Norton.

Haraway, D. (1988). Situated knowledges: The science question in feminism and the privilege of partial perspective. *Feminist Studies, 14*(3), 575–599. https://doi.org/10.2307/3178066

Hegel, G. W. F. (1807/1977). *Phenomenology of spirit* (A. V. Miller, Trans.). Oxford University Press.

Hegel, G. W. F. (1812/1969). *The science of* logic (A. V. Miller, Trans.). Allen & Unwin.

Hoerr, T. R. (2000). *Becoming a multiple intelligences school*. ASCD.

Kevles, D. J. (1998). *In the name of eugenics: Genetics and the uses of human heredity*. Harvard University Press.

Kitcher, P. (2011). *Science in a democratic society*. Prometheus Books.

Kornhaber, M. L., Fierros, E. G., & Veenema, S. A. (2004). *Multiple intelligences: Best ideas from research and practice*. Pearson.

Ladson-Billings, G. (2014). Culturally relevant pedagogy 2.0: Aka the remix. *Harvard Educational Review, 84*(1), 74–84. https://doi.org/10.17763/haer.84.1.p2rj131485484751

Lemann, N. (1999). *The big test: The secret history of the American meritocracy*. Farrar, Straus and Giroux.

Lipman, P. (2004). *High-stakes education: Inequality, globalization, and urban school reform*. Routledge.

Manning, C. D., Raghavan, P., & Schütze, H. (2008). *Introduction to information retrieval*. Cambridge University Press.

Newell, A., & Simon, H. A. (1976). Computer science as empirical inquiry: Symbols and search. *Communications of the ACM, 19*(3), 113–126. https://doi.org/10.1145/360018.360022

Noble, S. U. (2018). *Algorithms of oppression: How search engines reinforce racism*. NYU Press.

Reardon, S. F. (2011). The widening academic achievement gap between the rich and the poor: New evidence and possible explanations. *Community Investments, 23*(2), 19–39.

Rogoff, B. (2003). *The cultural nature of human development*. Oxford University Press.

Rose, T. (2016). *The end of average: How we succeed in a world that values sameness*. HarperOne.

Selwyn, N. (2019). *Should robots replace teachers? AI and the future of education.* Polity Press.
Snider, A. C., & Schnurer, M. (2006). *Many sides: Debate across the curriculum.* IDEA Press.
Sorensen, T., Jiang, L., Hwang, J. D., Levine, S., Pyatkin, V., West, P., Dziri, N., Lu, X., Rao, K., Bhagavatula, C., Sap, M., Tasioulas, J., & Choi, Y. (2024, March). Value kaleidoscope: Engaging AI with pluralistic human values, rights, and duties. In *Proceedings of the AAAI Conference on Artificial Intelligence, 38*(18), 19937–19947. https://arxiv.org/abs/2309.00779v2
Sousa, D. A. (2016). *How the brain learns* (5th ed.). Corwin.
Sternberg, R. J. (1985). *Beyond IQ: A triarchic theory of human intelligence.* Cambridge University Press.
Tomlinson, C. A., & McTighe, J. (2006). *Integrating differentiated instruction and understanding by design: Connecting content and kids.* ASCD.
Turing, A. M. (1950). Computing machinery and intelligence. *Mind, 59*(236), 433–460. https://doi.org/10.1093/mind/LIX.236.433
U.S. Congress. (2002). *No Child Left Behind Act of 2001*, Pub. L. No. 107–110, 115 Stat. 1425.
Visser, B. A., Ashton, M. C., & Vernon, P. A. (2006). Beyond g: Putting multiple intelligences theory to the test. *Intelligence, 34*(5), 487–502. https://doi.org/10.1016/j.intell.2006.02.004
Waterhouse, L. (2006). Multiple intelligences, the Mozart effect, and emotional intelligence: A critical review. *Educational Psychologist, 41*(4), 207–225. https://doi.org/10.1207/s15326985ep4104_1

CHAPTER 7

Artificial Intelligence and the City

G. Thomas Goodnight

Abstract Artificial Intelligence and the City investigates how accelerating AI deployment is reshaping urban governance, knowledge production, and everyday life. Building on Demis Hassabis's warning that society is "not ready" for AGI, I situate cities as primary arenas where readiness is negotiated through the emergence of epistemic communities—dense networks of officials, experts, citizens, and machines that practice "knowledge diplomacy." Tracing the Hiroshima G-7 process and other norm-setting efforts, the essay compares three regulatory imaginaries: European rights-based, U.S. market-oriented, and Chinese authoritarian. It distinguishes "smart" cities that harness IoT data for efficiency from "intelligent" cities that allow AI to steer planning, and projects that by 2030 at least half of major urban centers will embed AI in core public functions. Using rhetorical lenses of topics and loci, I analyze how AI now mediates urban concerns such as mobility, health, waste, environment, and infrastructure while interacting with everyday common-sense judgment. Philosophical traditions—from Aristotle's protreptic rhetoric to Deweyan pragmatism—frame a call for deliberative feedback loops aligning machine inference with human values. Ultimately, the study contends

G. T. Goodnight (✉)
21st Century Forensics, University of Southern California, Los Angeles, CA, USA
e-mail: gtg@usc.edu

P. A. Rao (ed.), *AI Pluralism*,
https://doi.org/10.1007/978-3-032-06558-2_7

that plural, commonsense-oriented epistemic communities can temper existential risks, bridge North–South digital divides, and steer AI toward truly resilient, more sustainable, humane, culturally inclusive, and globally just urban futures.

Keywords AGI readiness • Common sense • Digital divide • Epistemic communities • Hiroshima • G-7 • Intelligent cities • Knowledge diplomacy • Market-oriented model • Mobility management • Norm-setting • Pragmatism • Protreptic rhetoric • Rights-based regulation • Smart cities • Sustainable futures • Topics and loci • Urban Governance • Urban resilience

Google DeepMind CEO Demis Hassabis (2025) warns: "AGI Is Coming, Society's Not Ready." This conjecture assumes that societies cannot learn quickly enough to use AI well and avoid its risk. Human "readiness" is the question at hand. The international process of establishing norms for global regulation began to take these issues up at the Hiroshima G-7 conference in 2023 (OECD-AI, n.d.; Hiroshima AI, 2024). Norms continue to be debated, even as AI development accelerates across the planet. There are existential risks to unfettered substitutions of artificial for human intelligence. However, cities across the globe are now assembling powerful ways of understanding, controlling, and adjusting to Artificial Intelligence. This essay illustrates how epistemic communities are taking off at an exponential rate. Epistemic communities advance human readiness by evolving theory and practice. Rhetorical efforts tie proleptic principles to pragmatic deliberation. Deliberation is the soul of epistemic communities that conduct knowledge diplomacy at the local, regional, and international levels of power.

Cities are the inventions of civilizations going back five millennia. The world's cities constitute vast experiments in sustainable living and resilient response to disruptions. Every city is vulnerable. The knowledge of its residents must adapt, adjust, and grow incrementally to ongoing changes. A socio-technical imaginary develops to accommodate changes. Sometimes cities thrive by seeking intelligence outside the limits of its own embedded epistemic order. New ways of doing things with novel technologies create appropriate change. Knowledge may be ordered and comfortable, even if imperfect, for a time. City residents and leaders come up against the unknown, the misestimated, chaotic patterns of change. With AI, the multitude begins to deal in complicated ways with vast amounts of useful data as well as disinformation contagions (Lee et al., 2024).

In 2014, the World Economic Forum announced a push toward AI. Nations and corporations began planning for the transformation. Automated representational knowledge and robotics were included in this effort. In 2023, CHAT-GPT announced its availability to the public. Cities began rapidly adopting AI to service areas such as traffic management, utilities, and public services. Chat-GPT (2025) estimates that 15 to 25% of major cities will have AI commitments by 2030. ANTHROPIC Claud (2025) is more optimistic. "By 2030, over half of the world's cities will use AI for public functions." AI conferences, conventions, and advertising announce, promote and evaluate growing hosts of new products, relevant to city uses. This essay illustrates how societies build systems of governance and ethics. Epistemic communities take up this work at the local, city, county, state, and international levels. This ordering of AI is inherently pluralistic, we argue. Cities work to initiate AI in rights-based (Europe), market- oriented (United States), and authoritarian (China Belt and Road) societies across the globe. The urban scenes constitute a vortex of change. Communication bubbles, institutional spheres of actions, and networked infrastructures rush to couple Artificial Intelligence and the twenty-first-century city. The period of transition North and South is turbulent. Common sense, pragmatic inquiries circle our changing cities.

7.1 The Processes of Inquiry: AI and City Dwellers

Chat-GPT extrapolates: "By 2030, over half of the world's cities will use AI for public functions." In the Global North there is likely to be a 70 to 80% adoption rate. Southern urban centers will have a 40–50%. Overall, the market for smart cities grows larger in a post-COVID- 19 world. AI is limited by the availability of material resources, energy, information workers, and financial capital. Local, pragmatic factors apply, too. Different models of Artificial Intelligence offer expansive systems. Cities will have to match resources, goals, and politics to systems that are judged to be most effective, least costly, compatible with current infrastructure, and safe.

Leaders, managers, and experts are recruited to learn AI work procedures and usefulness. City residents are beginning the long process of learning what, how, whether, and at what cost to address AI systems. For example, The Bloomberg Philanthropies City Data Alliance now includes 65 cities across 12 countries. New mayors will receive operational support. The alliance works at "upskilling" everyone at city hall (Bloomberg Philanthropies City Data Alliance, 2025). The alliance was designed to grow significantly, with a total of 100 cities expected to join the City Data Alliance over the next two years. Internet tools and investments paved the way for the transition to computer science systems of information control. IBM (2025) has similar training ambitions for city administrators as well as experts that carry out knowledge functions in institutions such as business, health, and security. The cost of replacing humans with information mechanisms is unknown, but growth and investment continue anyway.

Knowledge generation and inquiry expand with great force within and across cities. The propinquity of residents, the density of people, the mobility of commuters—all these complex functions require infrastructure. Infrastructure, in turn, requires information services. Service changes require accountable judgment. Simultaneously with the technological advance, human understanding, expectations, and problem identification morph and grow. After all, cities are vast centers of human cooperation in learning: How do we live together, peacefully and well?

AI offers new ways of doing things with communication at the personal, professional, and public levels. AI experiences vary; so, judgment is crucial. What, if any, AI technologies are to be tried out, imitated, assembled, and woven into everyday patterns of exchange? What is the proper balance of human and AI authority, given the mission of an institution in service of a population? Rhetorical propositions that address general issues at specific sites are vital in a time of change. A rhetoric of inquiry investigates propositions of action. To do or undo? That is the question.

7.2 AI and Practices: Topics and Loci of Action

AI provides rapid improvement to computer strategies of virtual cognition. "The global number of AI tools users in the 'AI Tool Users' segment of the Artificial Intelligence market was forecast to continuously increase between 2025 and 2031 by in total 826.2 million (+238.59 percent). After the tenth consecutive increasing year, the number of AI tools users is estimated to reach 1.2 billion" (Statista Research Department, 2025). As a consequence elite commitments, some 7 billion human nonusers will have to learn how to advance their own learning to resist, adapt, hack, or avoid these tools. Many people may want the tools, but not have access; others, resist. This evolving knowledge production mix is transitory—even chaotic. Inquiry is complex. Individuals name, identify, and articulate reasons for actions of human agents. Topics and loci emerge for discussions that articulate needs, events, and necessities. Topics focus attention. Loci spark local action into being. Remember that approximately half the world populations live at the edge of poverty or below. The city sustains inequalities in networks of communication.

AI and city processes find partnerships in topics that address general situations and specific loci articulate the needs and resources for an area. This study identifies the grounds of a philosophy of the city. Choices are made for practical reasons; however, each decision takes a protreptic leap to extend principles. Principles can affirm, question, or oppose actions. Common sense is pragmatic, most of the time. Corrections are built into social structures when common- sense judgments are unavailable to an individual. Presently, AI is deployed as an unnoticed companion to city residents and visitors (Maese, 2025). Humans must determine the negative, when knowledge tools aren't working or are not worth the cost. Ordering is a function of AI (McCord, 2025). The "Smart City" was offered as a modern wonder. It was to be the glorious arena of sustainable growth for international network society.

7.3 The Smart City and the Intelligent City: Models and Transitions

The "smart city" is a great symbolic invention that positions AI as an assembly of tools to make an urban area run better. After all, the city has been the site of digital network extensions, and it is where AI is making many of its greatest impacts. The smart city is a term that refers to the connection of city services to the Internet of Things (IoT). The use of data permits real-time city adjustment to its operations, planning, and daily problem interventions. The intelligent city goes beyond thinking of Artificial Intelligence as an augmentation of routine systems; rather, AI connects systems by controlling data and the planning processes. The concepts of smart and intelligent cities are strong terms that promote computer science and digital networks of expertise. Cities do have access to mathematical techniques, computational machinery, and software specialists. Influencers and advertisers are at work selling products to users.

Smart Cities played a role in global development. These efforts were put into play prior to Covid-19. New cities are planned and old city districts remodeled to meet local needs and sustainable goals (Roth & Incera, 2024). In sum: "Smart Cities leverage technology to enhance urban living, focusing on data-driven decision-making, sustainability, and improved public services. On the other hand, Intelligent Cities emphasize the importance of human capital, fostering innovation, and creating a knowledge-based economy" (Inam, 2024). Cities are put in a competitive relationship to one another through global ranking systems. For example, "The IMD Smart City Index 2024 evaluates the perceptions of urban residents regarding their cities' infrastructure and technological solutions. It ranks 142 cities worldwide, offering a comprehensive view of urban development and innovation" (TPBO, 2024).

The differences between supplemental and decision-making AI technologies are stark. "While smart cities focus on efficiency and automation using technology, intelligent cities emphasize addressing community-specific challenges and fostering innovation from the ground up" (Inam, 2024). Hegemons compete by offering models of city success and AI. As we have seen, a single city model does not comport symmetrically with the complex pluralistic needs, features, and building of historic and new cities across the globe. How are cities most likely to build, refresh, or transition the wealth of common sense that sustains the judgments of their visitors, transients, and residential populations through good times and bad? Smart city advertising glistens with promises. However, AI in many places has a trust gap (Chakravorty, 2024). In particular, AI systems are associated with propaganda, disinformation, and state control (Ryan-Mosely, 2023; Swiatecki, 2025). Credibility requires routes to a built-in ethics and governance that work toward the common good.

Every city on the planet performs daily a host of planned and unplanned experiments in cooperative and competitive living. Cities do borrow from one another. Urban administration, planning and work experiences are catalogued by professionals who provide expert knowledge of opportunities and necessities facing people of the varied legal zones and local ecologies of a greater city area. Each city has a specific history, a relationship with its residents, a location within a sovereign (or failed) state. Artificial Intelligence is a new, popular assembly of techniques; however, it is costly, not reliable, and in the process of development. Cities will have to respond to national governments and decide what assemblies of Artificial Intelligence are to be installed, modified, repaired, and connected in what manner. In this book, Professor Hines points out that these are pragmatic questions that require attention to local knowledge and are historically conflicted because cities host opposing elements that become voiced in different ways.

7.4 The City as Context and AI for Knowledge Development

Cities are spaces where new knowledge boils constantly. The city has the resources for the specialization of actors. Cities are known for universities where basic research and practical knowledge contribute to advances in solving problems and providing an expert workforce for the city's being. However, practices of city workers extend to practical judgments. Data supplements. Information is manipulated in ways that simulate or model reality, knowledge, or action. The virtual may or may not resemble existential realities defined by intersubjective human understanding. Human deliberative practices require a veridical adjustment of effort, experience, interpretation with expectation, repertoires of action, and review. Practices furnish the grounds of city living where local bubbles, institutional spheres, and public gatherings. Consider cities as an ongoing reservoir of building and testing common sense. Contemporary cities have added (in different ways) systems thinking to common sense by building and repairing infrastructures for the common good.

7.4.1 Ancient Cities

Modern archaeologists appreciate the city as a socio-technical entity that provides a window into the social imaginary that supported the life-world of residents at home in one place and traveling to others. Buildings, roads, and green spaces comprise ancient cities. The study of ancient civilizations has been aided by Artificial Intelligence analysis (Vina, 2024). What is most difficult to extrapolate, however, is the common sense that pulsed through the everyday life of the people. Anthropologist Clifford Geertz maintained that "common sense is historically contingent, culturally constructed and in need of inquiry" (Archaeology of Common Sense, 2015). Cities are built atop structures from the past. The moment-to-moment, living common sense that vitalizes the life of the residents, institutions, and people—all these remain a matter to be "recovered" by inquiry into localities and the remains of structures and artifacts. Likewise, the analysis of AI can take an archeological orientation to the use of digital tools, even while extrapolating what appear to be common-sense examples, rules, norms, or general practices of older peoples. AI is also useful in analyzing village comportment and town networks.

7.4.2 Modern Cities

Over the last 200 years, modern cities have come to dot the globe. Capital cities grew with the Industrial Revolution. Planned urban areas began largely in the West. Science and technology were harbingers of progress. Population pressures continued to expand. Urban populations grew. The number of cities proliferated. Concentrated living arrangements provided centers for gathering of workers at factories, and shoppers at department stores. Families showed up at gatherings. Eventually, those with special needs were accommodated, and transients to hang out.

The city is a site of constant mobility. Residents come and go within the daily routines of the commute. Poor and wealthy visitors venture to the city. An entertaining visit for some is a desperate act of migration for others. Street systems organize mobility and structure city districts. "In 1980, 2.3 billion people lived in cities, about 40% of the global population. By 2080, 9.3 billion people will be living in cities, about 80% of the world's population. A doubling of the percentage and a quadrupling of the number of people living in cities. And if you take cities of 1 million or more over that period, we're going from about 275 cities to 1600 cities, which is a multiplication by six" (Colclough, 1923). Modern cities underwent transitions in the late twentieth century, when freeways and digital communications entered the scene through Internet connections. The Internet was first announced as the knowledge highway.

7.4.3 The Twenty-First-Century City

The twenty-first-century will furnish homes for Artificial Intelligence projects amid times of population movements, varied life-worlds, and accelerating transitions from climate change to pop-up civil strife and displacements. Our new city must shoulder the burden of blending old and new infrastructure in sustainable ways. Further, post COVID-19 cities must build or refurbish measures that assure resilience. Cities now undergo unpredictable risks and interactive failures at increasing rates. AI develops more numerous and greater options for intervening into global exploration and extracting resources from the Arctic, the deep-sea beds, or the cosmos.

City populations differ by virtue of historical development, national relationships, networks, and infrastructures of population and trade. Cities may borrow technologies, but each has a unique mix of what it needs, wants, and money. The politics of the city and AI are complex. Advanced, global cities could use AI to maximize advantages through the efficient coordination of services. Paris, Berlin, London, and New York are considered to be the first modern global cities. Shanghai, Beijing, and Manila exhibit a recent shift of world leaders to the Global South and East. Each city is a complex, changing, unique configuration of knowledge inquiries, management, and resources. Day-to-day, the common sense of its governors and residents is called up to handle responsibilities and judgments.

Each city sustains institutions that configure norms of conduct for purposes of organization and security; each city maintains old infrastructure and creates new zones of work and play. For example, Manila preserves the older romantic port areas while upscaling and building new, attractive spaces for business and industry. The modern, industrial city is recrafted by advanced, real-time city planning. What once were assets have now become liabilities (e.g., old office buildings into new housing resources). The advantages of Artificial Intelligence are put to work through enhancing the appearance and uses of urban zones. The advanced state of Singapore has developed information techniques to match university offerings with projected employment needs. Lagos has recently implemented guidelines for Dyna.ai. The guidelines are promoted to keep AI mistakes from "becoming radioactive" problems for the industry (Whitehead, 2025).

7.5 Global North and Global South

The Brookings Institution observed that "AI is transforming the world" (West & Allen, 2018). The world is always changing, of course. Widespread use of AI is a relatively new phenomenon, however. Many predictions are made about the future, including the shocking idea that AI will outstrip human knowledge and produce a singularity (Kurzweil, 2024).

Speculations are one thing; the historical context for advancing sociotechnical knowledge systems is quite another. Every city may desire AI, but each has a distinctive culture, resources, governance structure, and citizen ethos. Remember that AI is a covering term for a host of technical enterprises that groups with the city may put to some purposes. Those in the Global North routinely have greater access to technology; others in the Global South will be restricted due to a lack of money, technology, and labor resources. Urban systems are coming to vary a great deal, depending upon whether data centers are located in the Global North or South (Satarino & Mozur, 2025). The digital gap will grow rapidly in the next 20 years. Consider the distinct geographically rooted forms of AI integration.

7.5.1 *The Global North*

AI can be understood from the perspective of a game-changing supplement to traditional problem-solving approaches for issues in areas of governance. AI works by rendering the waves of activity in the city more compatible with the capacities of infrastructures at different times of the day or in different seasons. AI acts as a supplement to city governance, and it can provide real-time responses to needs.

In the Global North, the examples of Artificial Intelligence use tend to fall into maximizing the value of modern infrastructures. Holland, for example, is making the most of AI with its water engineering. In the established cities of the Global North, AI is directed to secure efficiency. Predictive Traffic Management reduces congestion in several ways, for instance. In Austin Texas, for instance, predictions lead to commuter identification, traffic control, and pricing on toll roads. London and Los Angeles coordinate red lights.

Common sense and AI work in developed cities to sustain daily living. For example, in Los Angeles, energy prices vary according to peak and off-peak hours. Millions of city consumers get cheaper energy if they run energy-thirsty appliances at night. Further, varied prices are available for using less energy when heat waves form and energy needs are high.

Artificial Intelligence improves urban Health Monitoring. Such systems were in place in California and in Toronto during and through the phases of COVID-19. The sources could compute the spread of the various by tracking cell phone and other data across a local region. The monitoring and analysis of wastewater in urban areas lends predictive power to elements coming into play that may threaten public health. Toronto has analyzed responses to public health crises to learn how events unfold. The data on public response allows for better health. Trash, too, can be handled more efficiently. "AI-powered systems analyze real-time data to optimize waste collection routes, saving fuel and reducing emissions. Recycling Innovations: AI detects contaminants in recycling streams, improving the quality of recyclable materials" (Global Trash Solutions, 2025). Dumping trash, commitments to recycling, and community dispersal raise social justice issues and pragmatic value. Training is provided by access to the Internet and by getting away to special conventions. The county of Miami-Dade in Florida, for example, held training sessions so that its administrators could learn how to work with AI within and across unites (Cava, 2024; Report, n.d.).

7.5.2 The Global South

The development of cities across the Eastern and Southern quadrants of the globe exhibits great differences with their neighbors to the North and West. Leading cities in the Global South, particularly in Africa, South America, and South Asia, include Lagos, Johannesburg, and Cairo in Africa; Sao Paulo, Rio de Janeiro, and Buenos Aires in South America; and Delhi, Mumbai, and Dhaka in South Asia. "Countries throughout the Global South are embracing new cities to address the challenges of rapid urbanization and economic stagnation, and to foster solutions for social inclusion and environmental sustainability" (Klaus, 2023). Southern cities differ a good deal across regions. In developing countries, rural-to-city urbanization requires AI to evolve strategic models that work with slum mapping, local governance, informal economies, waste disposal, clean water availability, and local resident participation. Security, disease prevention, health availability are challenges. Common sense, participatory means of living characterize the large favela of Rio or the *ciudades perdidas* of Mexico City. The arrangement of living is not so much governed by external sources as produced in organic fashion, locally. "Pioneered in Curitiba, Brazil in the 1960s, eco cities aim to create a sustainable and livable environment for residents while reducing their impact on the planet" (Klaus, 2023). In newly imagined eco-cities, AI is adopted through grassroots organizations and non-governmental agencies to add to information gathering, data resources, and policy formations for sustainability practices (Okolo, 2023). "Common sense" as traditional cautions thus are changing to empowering arcs of discourse.

Urban areas lagging in modern development could use AI to make up for the gaps in technology and robust infrastructure. Modern progress has been uneven. Approximately 43 percent of the world's 8 billion people still live in rural areas. Approximately 800,000 million people live in either rural or urban poverty. Many of the poor are agricultural laborers. China searches for solutions to the oscillation of populations between city and village. The lessons are part of diplomacy. China has fostered leading "intelligent" cities, while at the same time working with cities in Africa to support growth (China's Smart Cities, 2024). The Global Cities Index provides a ranking of city qualities that provide inviting grounds for the benefits of AI.

7.5.3 Alliances and Hegemons

China, the European Union, and the United States are the largest centers of artificial development. Presently, these historic, social, and technical political economies of knowledge and communication are in flux. International networks facilitate greater pluralism. Capital investment, trade, and migration follow. For example, the BRICS network connects geographically diverse nations. Russia, India, China, and South Africa. Egypt, Ethiopia, Indonesia, Iran, and the United Arab Emirates joined as well. "Artificial intelligence is increasingly being adopted in major BRICS cities, notably impacting urban planning, public service management, and civic engagement" (Blanchet, 2025). Smart cities in the BRICS: Artificial Intelligence, South–South cooperation, and the future of sustainable urban development. Shanghai and Shenzhen are identified as smart cities in China.

Pluralism among cities—North and South—is not assured. The United States works with Star Link to influence OPEC nations, BRICS, and the UK to dominate the field of AI. China has substantially developed its cities, mobility, and universities. It works with the extended Belt and Road diplomacy, as well as Russia. The United Nations represents developing countries in promoting a cautious, ethical, rights-based approach to AI, as does the European Union.

Hegemons compete to deploy AI models. The United States is using tariffs and trade wars to pursue AI dominance. It has disarmed all its international soft-power resources, such as the popular AID program. China is promoting Belt and Road initiatives through credit and energy policies (2014–present). Philosophy offers principled thinking about what the future should hold.

7.6 Philosophy and the City: Classical and Modern Practical Reason

A global debate over Artificial Intelligence started up in 2024 (Pan et al., 2025). Good actors could use the new tool toward admirable ends; bad actors, too, are empowered to pursue self-advantage or do evil. In 2025, controversies build, but the race for AI dominance among nations captures headlines and capital. Discussions continue as practices unfold. The result is a pluralistic system of ordering AI. China has invested AI safety in party regulation, combined with state incentives for development and resources allocated to education. The United States promotes private development and voluntary, self-regulation. Europe works to create a middle course by advocating rights-based applications of AI. Meanwhile, thinkers are beginning to lay out whole new definitions of major concepts in a post-humanist world (Iapaolo & Lynch, 2025). Philosophy offers another layer of contentious speculation and reconceptualization. Philosophical critique may be helpful; however, we prefer to draw upon cultural resources, empirical examples, and understanding of practices. Two major traditions of philosophy and the city are presented.

7.6.1 *Protreptic Thinking*

Aristotle was a classical, teleological philosopher. He drew his observations on human intelligence from his observations of people in the city-state of Athens. There, debates took place in the city forum. Aristotle wrote an Ethics, Politics, and Rhetoric to illustrate the choices available in putting purpose to foreseeable, contingent ends. Aristotle also wrote a Protrepticus. Persuasion can offer winning recipes that augment public speech. However, Aristotle found persuasion to reach higher ends when the principles raised by its use were the product of reflection, consistency, and principle. Protreptic thinking articulated the values of moving from practical action to philosophical thinking (Walker, 2010). Protrepsis is a form of exhortation to act consistently upon the experiences, success, and limits of conduct. *Prolepsis* (a related trope) is a figure of thought whereby one anticipates likely objections—attributed to Aristotle in the *Rhetoric ad Alexandrum*. Protreptic thinking and proleptic strategies put the objects of action first, then contemplate the necessity of reflection and the value of strategic anticipation of objection. How would a critical thinker understand the uses of reason in the particular case and how are objections and opposition be taken into account? Reflective thought is produced by experiential generalizations. Philosophical questions can arise from rhetorical encounters. To achieve practical success, it is necessary to anticipate objections. Common sense, necessary for practical reason becomes tested in this process, I have found. Common sense for a community, for example, may be expressed as conventions. Conventions rule for a time. Eventually, some become dated or out of synch. Conventions are tested by common-sense informed decisions. The shared intersubjectivity of a resident versus a migrant, for example, stems from distinct readings of the necessity of actions upon a scene.

Aristotelean thinking held that words should be put to good purpose. The authority, emotional register, and the story needs align the audience with the occasion. The occasion could be a ritual observation for debate or it could be a special session called into being by urgencies to decide. The facts of the case were to be laid out in a case that argued for change to the projects of the polis. The term "pragmata" understands facts not to be points that are convertible to neutral data. Rather, facts are objects the experiencing of which afford a hook for use. Facts of the case were relevant to problem-solving decisions and social science testing for effects. Common sense underwrites practical intelligence that accords intelligent, tested purpose to action in behalf of the well-being of the city—Athens, before questions of empire overwhelmed its pieties.

7.6.2 Pragmatism

Pragmatism was a school of philosophy associated with the University of Chicago. John Dewey developed a logic of problem solving. A common problem constituted a public issue that could be resolved. For example, if a bridge is needed to connect workers with factories, its evidence will show not only how but also the benefits of a government initiation. William James, a psychologist, acknowledged the variety of genuine beliefs and blind spots from which human beings reasoned (James, 1899). Nevertheless, efficient labor invites cooperative activity, or working together. Finally, the semanticist Charles Pierce wrote of pragmatic focus as a way of wasting time on abstract issues of metaphysics. Rather, he invented the idea of "an infinite community of inquiry" (Rollins, 2022). This community of inquiry is, in principle, an infinite, evolving group who together strive to 'understand reality through shared inquiry and the pursuit of truth.' Pragmatism continues inclusive discussions by granting everyone a seat at the table. Different points of view may cast an alternative light on actions under deliberation. The city is a place for stakeholders who were instructed on how to recognize facts, needless inconvenience or suffering, and engage in the steps of problem solving (Dewey, 1910). Pragmatic thinking moved to drawn in alternative viewpoints, so that modern life of an immigrant-rich democracy could flourish (Pragma, 2023). Common talent needs cultivation through universal education. Thus, the cities were ruled by bosses, but communication encouraged acts of resistance, deliberative discussion, debate, and consensus. Pragmatic, evidence-based reasoning furnished the disciplined, inclusive architectonics of modern city life.

7.6.3 Rhetoric Furnishes the Beginnings of Artificial Intelligence

Rhetoric transformed ritual performance to techniques of defending an action in front of an audience. Peitho was the goal, thought the means, language the performance. For Aristotle, rhetoric was to be considered a practical guide to conduct. Rhetoric, ethics, and politics constituted a driving dynamic for the city in general. A particular any city could be studied for its particular constitutional form. The speaker addressed an audience called together on an occasion. Rhetoric identified the speaker with an intent to persuade using the best means at his disposal in order to dismiss the worst arguments of the day. Rhetorical technology is a process. Five cannons were followed to identify the process as a system of knowledge inquiries: invention, arrangement, style, memory, and action. Topics and loci relevant to an occasion, persuasive intention, or a problem present us with cultural materials. These materials are still in use. A rhetorical perspective brings together topics and loci with critical thinking to pursue the useful marriage of AI agencies and Human city residents together.

The individual user of AI needs to have a knowledge of topics and loci to engage in the process of "dialogue" with the apparatus. A topic is a general area of conversation where the individual starts with a limited, middle range, or rich amount of information. A locus is a particular place where the topic finds expression. A discussion can start with loci and move more generally to information about the topic over time or place.

7.7 Artificial Intelligence as a Deliberative Movement

City use of Artificial Intelligence has reached a take-off point. Most everyone seems persuaded to consider AI as the vibrant new reality. The world begins to spin in an AI action vortex. In 2023, "Only 2% of local governments are currently using AI, but more than two-thirds are exploring its potential" (Jackley, 2024). In 2025, New York Business Wire reported: "Cities around the world are racing to adopt AI to drive productivity and efficiency and boost their economies, according to a global study of 250 cities conducted by ServiceNow and Deloitte, in collaboration with ThoughtLab, a leading provider of thought leadership research" (Celi, 2025). AI and the City seem to be forming a powerful alliance. Human agents who provide city leadership, direct services, organize departments, provide citizens with information, and intervene in crises. AI and common sense connect necessarily through topics and loci that apperceive the shapes of objects and provide the means of intervention. AI feedback loops specify categories for description, evaluation, and consequences of outcomes (IBM & C40 Cities, 2025). From a protreptic point of view, a "feed back loop" is the proleptic consideration of positive or negative principles that apply to a case. Thinking supports deliberation. Deliberation emerges in a discourse of choice. At base, it requires a selection of topics and energized vectors of loci.

7.7.1 City Topics

City topics are drawn and assembled from vast discursive or information aggregations, since a mechanism may draw from general Internet resources or data pools. Urban topics relevant to AI include: (1) Questions of mobility that include traffic light coordination, peak hours of driving, accidents, and clean up. (2) Questions of medical care and disease that include monitoring illness, matching facilities and personnel to clinics and beds, controlling and targeting costs. (3) Waste and hazardous materials that include trash dumps, recycling, toxic dumps, clean ups. (4) Environmental concerns extend to clean air and water, chemical and waste regulation, and disaster relief and recovery. (5) Infrastructure issues that include housing provision and repair; systems that pipe water, gas, and electricity. Urban topics are not a finite set. Topics are discovered from both the history of a material area of known objectives of the city. Topics sometimes stem from operational definitions of abstract terms—such as equity. Different AI platforms will include or exclude particular issues from a range of standard topics. Practical reason demands critical thinking about the ways in which topics are ranked in relation to changing urgencies caused by mismatches of needs and resources.

7.7.2 *Urban Loci*

Urban loci refer to the common places of the city. Common places are available to experience. They can also be aggregated into groups and information extracted for other purposes of information. Yet, common places exist over time. There are an indefinite number of ways of examining them through a data extraction process. The local has significance for urban residents and city governance. Places require multiple points of connection, resources for safety and security, sales and supplies. Poor urban planning, such as that which ran freeways through the center of town, needs to be repaired. Unhealthy parts of the city beg for attention. Zones are fashioned to manage biomes whose governance changes over time.

Loci vary across scales. Loci can take up a disaster, like Houston's Hurricane Harvey. Loci evolve as part of an evolving story. Houston's hurricane became days of rain that flooded the city. There are always more topics to be added to local narratives. Humans and machines can set up priorities, to tell the story of an event or object, review disaster activities, evaluate the losses, and mourn. LLM models will spin out topics with ease, but the loci of place are more interesting. Artificial Intelligence narratives add analytic strength to city narratives. AI did a good job in opening comparative inquiry, when I requested it to compare Houston and Manila on hurricanes or strong typhoons. Novel comparisons of loci create opportunities to push inquiries across plural localities of telling difference.

Any city has brought together a field of loci. These places and attendant events are places where everyday practice occurs. These are gathered for discussions when urgencies appear. Critical thinking adds to the research when common sense provides a warning that something is incomplete, missing from the story. Data banks and AI searches aid the process of discovery, in pursuing the overlooked. The topics that appear relevant constitute windows into cultural resources (and limits). These resources feed new ideas for invention. A critique of topoi and loci (that a system is said to embed) is required. It takes time and experience to construct necessary, new common-sense boundaries for arrangements of co-production between AI and citizens (Crehan, 2016).

7.8 Epistemic Communities

AI constitutes a rhetoric that organizes topics and loci for city development. AI is a persuasive movement. We expect waves of change as AI systems attract investment and become a necessity upon which we all depend, in various ways. The question remains: How does society keep up with the new knowledge systems? Social change is accelerating through the formation of epistemic communities. These communities are the seeds for novel ecologies of knowledge to which my colleagues in this volume refer. I offer a definition of the idea, present and modify Richard Haas's modern idea to suit a rhetorical relation between AI inferential projects and the protreptic evolution of human common sense. The goal of the section is to acquaint you with protreptic practices that are already underway, perhaps accelerating at the same rate as the vast investment-fueled projects of chip structured AI. The practices are presented at the scale of global exchange of international groups of urban mayors and other leaders, the middle range spheres of knowing. These include leaders from think tanks and other civic organizations that explicate and evaluate AI change for certain topics and loci of activities. Finally, I illustrate a few of the many, many micro bubbles that float into foams that spurt up in different colors, textures, and containers around the planetary landscape. Epistemic communities accelerate global transitions from the past Holocene epoch to rapidly evolving, Anthropocene pluralistic forms of life in city living.

7.8.1 A Twenty-First-Century Concept of an Epistemic Community: A Gathering of People Who Work, Communicate, and Bind Knowledge Projects

"*Urban Epistemic Communities focus on sustainable projects, value diversity and difference at varied levels of scale. Such groups hybridize the tools of communication (across different levels of scale) in adapting to differences. Resilience is built through the gathering and adjusting the defenses and opportunities within and against the authority-fueled machinery of misinformation, non-transparent data, appropriated platforms, and infelicitous simulations. Epistemic communities respond to needs, resources and necessities of community life (proximate or extended) in which equity is at stake*" [emphasis mine]. The idea of epistemic communities borrows from the teleological and pragmatic traditions of philosophy and the city. It resists contemporary efforts to reduce epistemics to cognition, and cognition to essentialist, categorical thinking, The evolution of techniques is important, but mathematical techniques compete to align AI with the true, real, and telling experiences. Rather, epistemic communities emphasize the challenges of human agency to know through bridging the gap through abstractions typical of the disciplinary sciences and practical knowledge (*phronesis*)—the product of reason and the grounding experiences of reaching a *sensus communis*. A *dissensus communis* occurs when a resolution, proposal, or policy comes under dispute.

7.8.2 The Diplomacies of Epistemic Communities

Richard Haas invented the term epistemic community as a human enterprise where experts apply their specialized knowledge to resolving practical problems (Haas, 1992). Such groups have "four unifying characteristics."

> "a **shared set of normative and principled beliefs** which would provide a value-based rationale for the social action of community members;
>
> "**shared causal beliefs which are derived from their analysis of practices** leading or contributing to a central set of problems in their domain and which then serve as the basis for elucidating the multiple linkages between the possible policy actions and desired outcomes;
>
> "**shared notions of validity, i.e., intersubjective, internally defined criteria** for weighing and validating knowledge the domain of their expertise; and
>
> "**a common policy enterprise, or set of common practices** associated with a set of problems to which their professional competence is directed, presumably out of conviction that human welfare."

The norms of expert practices underwrite the existence of epistemic communities. These groups may be small and informal. Individuals may be unrelated but gather together to spin a message, technology, or social norm that matters. Small groups may gather to learn about and care for topics that cross a local scene. Groups may be large and professional. Evidence-based expertise shares norms that are expressed in the formal ruling groups of a field. Fields differentiate through debate legitimate from illegitimate use of virtual space and just distribution of costs and risks for service. Finally, relationships among the multitudes and elites energize spheres of diplomacy of power and knowledge. Thus, AI is constituted in the bubbles and foam of a multitude of local messages; the institutional decorum of adopters and resistors; and the macho-vectors of global politics of the biosphere. Slotterdijk (1999, 2004a, 2004b) provides lifeworld ordering of each level of scale.

7.9 Beginnings

Nobel Prize winner Geoffrey Hinton (2025)—the "godfather of AI"—believes that there are advancing odds that "AI will wipe humanity out in the next thirty years." This paper acknowledges risks to Artificial Intelligence. However, human intelligence is advancing commensurate with AI challenges. Common sense becomes articulated by the communicative labor of epistemic communities. Common sense becomes articulated by the communicative labor of epistemic communities, groups that build traditions of choice and judgement. Varied and changing AI bundles are being installed. Each bundle has a unique history, assembly of trajectories, and relationship with prior infrastructures. Epistemic communities are shaping up into the bubbles of idiosyncratic users, the assertions of the authority in institutional spheres, and the aspirations to global norms and information diplomacy. Of course, each city initiative, however robust, represents a bounded area for assemblies of AI systems. AI growth prompts the emergence of inquiry, the beginnings of knowledge acceleration.

The relationships between human agents and attributed machine agency are dialectical. Perhaps co-produced ecologies will stabilize. Yet, the evolutionary properties of common sense will continue to seek and search out means to recognize and dismiss exploitative schemes.

Humans are pragmatic, risk-taking, and harm-averse creatures. Thinking in the city generates everyday protreptic principles of broad adjustment to knowledge at hand. City dwellers choose ad hoc routes, for example, when a street feels unsafe or when a transit app's ETA just "doesn't add up." Safety and travel thinking constitutes the topic of mobility and the loci of a high crime area. Aristotle called this practical wisdom, or *phronesis*, the foundational appeal that positions speakers as trustworthy guides to action. Protreptic principled thinking and proleptic pragmatics join to supply epistemic communities with human evaluative tools for the usefulness of AI in urban contexts. The rhetoric extends to the ordering, arrangement, analysis, and action inferred by topi, loci, in the evolution of knowledge and material constraints.

Thinking through the principles of choice is encouraged by the complexities city life.

Common sense is useful, but limited. The downtown scene is a prototypical hybrid system where built infrastructure, social norms, and data flows intersect at pace. In a city, human routines, institutional rules, and sensor-driven algorithms already interlock: streetlights dim when sensors detect no traffic, apps reroute buses around congested blocks, and public-safety cameras flag unusual behavior. This lived hybridity makes the city both a testing ground and a metaphor for assemblies of changing human–AI partnerships. Alfred North Whitehead understood that knowledge changes as an interactive process with its objects of inquiry, which are studied (Whitehead, 1978 [1929]; Schrag, 2022).

Cities are diverse adapters for AI. Platform owners and their employees want to win by controlling information. The race for "dominance" that drives the ambitions of hegemons appears to be a trap. AI systems may become the backbone of authoritarian states. Publics are surveilled and restricted. AI's uneven beginning and its imagined uses work to accord it a mixed reputation. For instance, AI projects are becoming associated with state hacking and misinformation (Ryan-Mosely, 2023). Therefore, a critique of AI and targeted falsehood (propaganda) needs to be kept open. The building of epistemic communities assures that pluralistic resources are available to recognize the differences among productive and arbitrary AI–human relationships. AI accords city focused administration greater sovereignty than nationalist control for status and security.

The twenty-first-century cities are rocketing into numerous high-stakes transitions.

Growing, elite groups are quickly leading urban knowledge structures into Artificial Intelligence. Urban residents appear willing to add AI to digital communication practices. The geographic growth and decline of human population overall generate needs for new forms of intelligence to accord cities systems more sustainable and processes of living more resilient to change. The city is a home for Artificial Intelligence which, of necessity, follows a pluralistic skein of changes over time. As AI grows more accepted and powerful, common-sense questions will grow in sophistication, variety, and intelligence at varied levels of context. The singularity, doom, and totalizing hegemony are not in the future. To the contrary, AI and Urban partnerships grow into knowledge rich epistemic communities.

Taken together, the chapters in this volume define **AI pluralism** as both a *governance stance* and an *architectural pattern*—a way of building and evaluating intelligent systems that treat disagreement as generative rather than pathological. Across domains and disciplines, the contributors converge on a single claim: that intelligence, human or artificial, achieves legitimacy only when it is open to contestation and accountable to multiple perspectives. By grounding pluralism simultaneously in rhetorical argumentation, philosophical inquiry, and computational design, this book extends beyond familiar paradigms such as alignment, explainability, or compound AI. It introduces new operators for structured synthesis with traceable dissent, new protocols for deliberative mediation, and new evaluative metrics for civic and epistemic robustness. In doing so, it offers not merely a critique of monolithic AI but a practical roadmap for designing systems that can *reason together in difference*—a pluralistic foundation for the next generation of human–machine coexistence.

References

Archaeology of Common Sense. (2015). The Digital Archaeological Record. Part of: Society for American Archaeology 80th Annual Meeting, San Francisco, CA. https://core.tdar.org/collection/29533/the-archaeology-of-common-sense#:~:text=Rather%20than%20colloquial%20wisdom%2C%20Clifford,not%2C%20of%20reifying%20common%20sense

Blanchet, A. (2025). Smart cities in the BRICS: Artificial intelligence, South-South cooperation, and the future of sustainable urban development. *BRICS Brazil*. https://brics.br/en/news/articles/smart-cities-in-the-brics-artificial-intelligence-south-south-cooperation-and-the-future-of-sustainable-urban-development#:~:text=Artificial%20intelligence%20is%20increasingly%20being,particularly%20 in%20Shanghai%20and%20Shenzhen

Bloomberg Philanthropies City Data Alliance. (2025). *A new frontier in data: Upskilling everyone in city hall*. https://bloombergcities.jhu.edu/program/data-alliance

Cava, D. (2024). Note from Honorable Chairman Oliver G. Gilbert, III and Members, Board of County Commissioners Daniella Levine Cava Mayor.

Celi, L. (2025). Cities embrace traditional and generative AI to become future-ready, new research finds. *Newswire*. Thoughtlab. https://www.businesswire.com/news/home/20250224300013/en/Cities-embrace-traditional-and-generative-AI-to-become-future-ready-new-research-finds

Chakravorty, B. (2024). AI's trust problem. *Harvard Business Review*. https://hbr.org/2024/05/ais-trust-problem

CHAT GPT. Open AI. (2025). Personal inquiry.
China's Smart Cities in Africa: Should the United States be concerned? (2024). Center for Strategic and International Studies. Jason Warner and Toyosi Ajibade. https://www.csis.org/analysis/chinas-smart-cities-africa-should-united-states-be-concerned#:~:text=China%20is%20encouraging%20the%20adoption,being%20developed%20with%20Chinese%20suppo
Claud, A. (2025). Personal inquiry.
Colclough, A. (1923). The century of cities—Interview. *Eurocities*. https://eurocities.eu/latest/cities-wont-run-the-world-interview/
Crehan, K. (2016). *Gramsci's common sense: Inequality and its narratives*. Duke University Press. https://doi.org/10.1215/9780822373742
Dewey, J. (1910). *How we think*. D.C. Heath and Company.
Global Trash Solutions. (2025). How AI is transforming waste management. https://globaltrashsolutions.com/blog/how-ai-is-transforming-waste-management/#:~:text=Yes%2C%20AI%2Dpowered%20systems%20with,is%20AI%20changing%20the%20environment?
Gregoric, P. (2007). *Aristotle on the common sense*. Oxford University Press. ISBN 9780199277377.
Haas, P. M. (1992). Introduction: Epistemic communities and international policy coordination. *International Organization. Cambridge Journals, 46*(1), 1–35.
Hassabis, D. (2025). Google deep mind. *NDTV*. https://www.ndtv.com/science/google-deepmind-ceo-on-what-keeps-him-up-at-night-agi-is-coming-societys-not-ready-8245874
Hinton, G. (2025). Godfather of AI' shortens odds of the technology wiping out humanity over next 30 years. https://www.theguardian.com/technology/2024/dec/27/godfather-of-ai-raises-odds-of-the-technology-wiping-out-humanity-over-next-30-years
Hiroshima AI Process: Leading the global challenge to shape inclusive governance for Generative AI. (2024). KIZUNA: The Government of Japan. https://www.japan.go.jp/kizuna/2024/02/hiroshima_ai_process.html#:~:text=The%20rapid%20development%20and%20spread,the%20foundation%20of%20such%20governance
Iapaolo, F., & Lynch, C. R. (2025). Rethinking urban AI: A critical posthumanist perspective on intelligence, autonomy, and agency. *Urban Geography*. https://doi.org/10.1080/02723638.2025.2510812
IBM. (2025). What is the smart city? https://www.ibm.com/think/topics/smart-city#:~:text=A%20smart%20city%20is%20an%20urban%20area,(ICT)%20and%20the%20Inter net%20of%20Things%20(IoT)
IBM & C40 Cities collaborate on new AI project for resilient cities. (2025). https://www.c40.org/news/ibm-and-c40-cities-collaborate-on-new-ai-project-for-resilient-cities/#:~:text=IBM%20and%20C40%20Cities%2C%20a,the%20urban%20heat%20island%20effect

Inam, M. (2024). Minnovation technologies. Smart city vs. intelligent city: Key differences and similarities.

Jackley, M. (2024). *Using AI in local government: 10 use cases.* Kunstmatge Intelligent. OCI.

James, W. (1899). On a certain blindness in human beings. https://monadnock.net/james/blindness.html

Klaus, E. (2023). *Emerging horizons: The rise of new cities in the Global South.* Charter Cities Institute. https://chartercitiesinstitute.org/blog-posts/rise-of-new-cities/#:~:text=Morocco%2C%20Kuwait%2C%20and%20Algeria%20have,the%20region%20has%20been%20slow

Kurzweil, R. (2024). *The singularity is nearer: When we merge with AI.* Penguin Publishing Group.

Lee, N. T., West, D. M., & Dunn K. M. (2024). *How do artificial intelligence and disinformation impact elections?* Brookings Center for Technology Information. https://www.brookings.edu/articles/how-do-artificial-intelligence-and-disinformation-impact-elections/

Maese, E. (2025). Americans use AI in everyday products without realizing it. *Gallup Social and Policy Issues.* https://news.gallup.com/poll/654905/americans-everyday-products-without-realizing.aspx#:~:text=Perceived%20usage%20of%20AI%20is,cities%20(44%25%2C%20vs

McCord, B. (2025). *The philosophical roots of decentralized AI.* Cosmos Institute. https://cosmos-institute.org/

OECD-AI. (n.d.) G7 reporting framework—Hiroshima AI Process (HAIP) international code of conduct for organizations developing advanced AI systems. https://transparency.oecd.ai/

Okolo, C. T. (2023). *AI in the Global South: Opportunities and challenges towards more inclusive governance.* Brookings Institute. https://www.brookings.edu/articles/ai-in-the-global-south-opportunities-and-challenges-towards-more-inclusive-governance/

Pan, S., Goodnight, G. T., Zhao, X., Wang, Y., Xie, L., & Zhang, J. (2025). Game changer: The AI advocacy discourse of 2023. *AI & Soviety, 40*(4), 2807–2819. https://doi.org/10.1007/s00146-024-02027-6

Pragma, A. (2023). Pragmatism and feminism: Epistemological, social, and political spaces of resistance. *European Journal of Pragmatism and American Philosophy, 15*, 1.

Report (n.d.) on Miami-Dade County's Policy on Artificial Intelligence—Directive No. 231203. Report on Miami-Dade's County on Artificial Intelligence.

Rollins, G. M. (2022). Charles Peirce and the community of inquiry. *Analytic teaching and Philosophical praxis, 43*(1), 1–16.

Roth. Z., & Incera M. (2024). *The rise of AI-powered smart cities.* S&P Global. https://www.spglobal.com/en/research-insights/special-reports/ai-smart-cities

Ryan-Mosely, T. (2023). How generative AI is boosting the spread of disinformation and propaganda. *MIT Technology Review*. https://www.technologyreview.com/2023/10/04/1080801/generative-ai-boosting-disinformation-and-propaganda-freedom-house/

Satarino, A. & Mozur, P. (2025). The global A.I. divide. Where A.I. data centers are located. *The New York Times*. https://www.nytimes.com/interactive/2025/06/23/technology/ai-computing-global-divide.html?smid=nytcore-ios-share&referringSource=articleShare

Schrag, C. O. (2022). *Whitehead: Process and reality*. EBSCO Research Starters Data Base. https://www.ebsco.com/research-starters/literature-and-writing/process-and-reality-alfred-north-whitehead#:~:text=%22Process%20and%20Reality%22%20is%20a,dynamic%20processes%20o ver%20static%20structures

Slotterdijk, P. (1999). *Bubbles: Spheres Volume I: Microspherology* (German: Sphären. Mikrosphärologie. Band I. Blasen) was published by Suhrkamp Verlag in 1998.

Slotterdijk, P. (2004a). *Globes: Spheres Volume II: Macrospherology* (German: Sphären. Makrosphärologie. Band II. Globen) was published by Suhrkamp Verlag in 1999.

Slotterdijk, P.(2004b). Foams: Spheres Volume III: Plural Spherology (German: Sphären. Plurale Sphärologie. Band III.

Statista Research Department. (2025, April 7). Number of artificial intelligence (AI) tool users globally from 2021 to 2031. https://www.statista.com/forecasts/1449844/ai-tool-users-worldwide

Swiatecki, C. (2025). *Council looks to expand AI policies, examine energy and water needs for data centers*. Austin Monitor.

TPBO. (2024). Smart city index: 2024. https://placebrandobserver.com/smart-city-index-2024-summary/

Vina, A. (2024). AI in archeology paves the way for new discoveries. *Ultralytics*. Yolo II. https://www.ultralytics.com/blog/ai-in-archaeology-paves-the-way-for-new-discoveries#:~:text=preserving%20our%20history.-,How%20computer%20vision%20is%20used%20in%20archaeology,and%20interpreting%20arc haeological%20findings%20easier

Walker, M. (2010). *The utility of contemplation in Aristotle's Protrepticus*. Philosophical Papers.

West, D. M., & Allen, J. R. (2018). *How Artificial Intelligence is transforming the world*. Brookings Institution. https://www.brookings.edu/articles/how-artificial-intelligence-is-transforming-the-world/

Whitehead, A. N. (1978). *Process and reality: An essay in cosmology*. Macmillan, 1929; corr.ed., In D. R. Griffin & D. W. Sherburne (Eds.). Free Press.

Whitehead, S. (2025). Lagos to unveil Nigeria's first AI guidelines. iAfrica. https://iafrica.com/lagos-to-unveil-nigerias-first-ai-guidelines-in-push-for-responsible-innovation/#:~:text=Alake%20described%20the%20guidelines%20as,consequences%20for%20 developers%20and%20companies

Index

P. A. Rao (ed.), *AI Pluralism*,
https://doi.org/10.1007/978-3-032-06558-2

Kolibri 360 GmbH
Ferdinand-Jühlke-Straße 7
99095 Erfurt, Deutschland
produktsicherheit@kolibri360.de